C000152977

A Pilgrim's Guide to
ROME and ASSISI

with other Italian Shrines

By Raymond Goodburn

Pilgrim Book Services Limited

Published by Pilgrim Book Services Ltd., P.O. Box 27, Woodbridge, Suffolk, England IP13 9AU

 www.pilgrimbooks.com

Designed by Bob Vickers
Cover design by Fielding Design
Maps by Rodney Paull
Production by Navigator Guides

Printed in Great Britain by Colourstream Litho Ltd.

 Mixed Sources
Product group from well-managed forests and other controlled sources
www.fsc.org   Cert no. SGS-COC-004224
© 1996 Forest Stewardship Council

Cover picture: St Peter

CONTENTS

A General Audience in St Peter's Square (© *L'Osservatore Romano – Servizio Fotografico*)

Part 1
PREFACE

Those already familiar with the 'Pilgrim's Guide' series may wonder why there should be a separate book on Rome and Assisi. Should it not be part of the previous book in the series, 'A Pilgrim's Guide to the Lands of St. Paul', which concentrates on Greece, Turkey, Malta and Cyprus? Why was Italy not also included?

One answer is that of sheer practicality and size. The aim of the 'Pilgrim's Guide' series is to provide the Christian visitor, of whatever church background, be it Catholic or Protestant, with information in a concise and portable manner. They are intended as handy reference books which can be read easily on a plane or coach, or even in a hotel room! Hopefully they will whet the appetite for further reading. All being well, by providing just the right amount of information about the various sites they will be an invaluable aid to the pilgrim on the move as well as a useful and colourful momento of places visited.

There is a second and more important reason. Given the historic significance of Rome as capital of the Roman Empire and therefore as the heart of the Gentile world into which Christianity spread from Jerusalem, a separate volume seemed appropriate. Though Rome, both ancient and modern, is the main focus of the book, many visitors to the city, either as individuals or with organised groups, will also want to visit Assisi. Such scope demands a book in its own right. As previously, it does not set out to be a comprehensive guidebook but rather to concentrate on those areas and sites which are most likely to appeal to the pilgrim. At the same time it highlights some of the artistic and architectural features which he or she may also want to explore.

For the Christian pilgrim to the 'Eternal City' the figures of St. Paul and St. Peter will rightly loom large. But a pilgrimage can never just be a re-visiting of history and its personalities. It is also a challenge to explore Christian truth and faith within the setting of the contemporary world, inspired by the insights of those who have gone before us.

Raymond Goodburn
2010

The Last Judgement by Michelangelo

Part 2
CHRISTIAN ROME
The Historical Setting

Not without reason is Rome frequently referred to as the 'Eternal City'. There is a large measure of agreement which dates its foundation to 753 BC and, indeed, there are those who would even suggest a precise date, 21 April. Prior to that date, however, a number of small villages appear to have existed in the region. According to legend, Rome as such was established on that date by Romulus and Remus, the twin sons of the Vestal virgin Rhea and the god Mars, the boys being brought up on the Palatine Hill (one of the seven hills which now form Rome) and cared for by a she-wolf. It was Romulus who duly gave his name to the city and set himself up as its first king, having killed Remus in a family feud.

By far the most important influence on the emerging city at this time was that of the **Etruscans** (616–509 BC), powerful neighbours living in the north and gradually expanding their influence southwards towards the Tiber. They were a much more advanced civilisation and under their direction Rome developed as a major city, with the various Etruscan kings residing there. As well as building the city walls they were also responsible for the Great Drain, the Cloaca Maxima sewers, which were necessary to drain the marshlands so that the Forum could be built.

But things were to change. Although the Etruscans had much to offer, the Romans came to resent their domination and in 509 BC the last of Rome's seven kings, Tarquin the Proud (Tarquinius Superbus), was dethroned and the **Roman Republic** founded.

For nearly 500 years, from 509–23 BC, the Republic was governed by the Senate and its assembly, though there was constant friction between the ruling classes *(the patricians)* and the lower classes *(the plebeians)*, the latter having their interests overseen by the office of the tribune. Considerable power was invested in certain officials, in particular the consuls. They exercised authority in much the same way as the previous kings, dealing with legislation, the judiciary and the military. There were always two consuls in office, with the one having the power of veto over the other. As a safeguard against dictatorship, consuls ruled for only one year, though they could be re-elected. Such a system of annual appointments meant that on the whole the consuls ruled rather conservatively and without a great deal of creativity. That said, however, the period of the Republic ushered in a great expansion of Roman power and civilisation, gradually conquering the rest of Italy and its Mediterranean neighbours in spite of a setback when the Gauls invaded Italy and sacked Rome in 390 BC. This was also the period of the three Punic Wars (264–146 BC) as Rome's expansion inevitably resulted in conflict with Carthage. Yet at the end of these wars, notwithstanding a defeat by Carthage and Hannibal in the second war, Rome dominated the Mediterranean including also, by 63 BC, the Holy Land.

But it was the continuing internal factions which led to the demise of the Republic and the rise of Julius Caesar. It was he who had to pull the nation together again in the aftermath of civil strife by means of a popular dictatorship, yet even that was too much for some and on the Ides of March, 15 March 44 BC, he was assassinated.

However, prior to his death, Caesar appointed Octavius as his son and heir and, ruling as Augustus, he was to do much to restore Rome and in 27 BC claimed for himself the title 'Emperor'. So began the great third period of Roman history after the Etruscans and the Republic, the mighty **Roman Empire,** which in political, cultural and religious terms was to become the very centre of the known world. Ruling as Augustus Caesar (27 BC–AD 14), he ushered in the zenith of Roman civilisation. It was he who laid the foundations of imperial Rome, the remains of which can still be seen by the contemporary visitor to the city. Perhaps few of his successors achieved quite what he did.

But it was this period of Roman history which had such profound significance for the birth, expansion and eventual acceptance of the new religion, Christianity. After all St. Luke, in his two volume work Luke-Acts, is anxious to show that not only was Christ born into the world at the time of Augustus but also that this was of more than mere local passing interest. Though he begins his Gospel in Jerusalem as the centre of the Jewish world, he is eager to remind his readers of the relevance of Christ's birth to the whole of Caesar's world, with the Acts of the Apostles ending in Rome, the centre of the Gentile world and the capital of the Empire. Jesus, as well as being the glory of Israel, is also a light to the Gentiles (Luke 2:32).

However, it was during the reign of Tiberius (AD 14–37), the successor of Augustus, that Jesus' ministry, crucifixion and resurrection took place. Caligula followed (37–41) during which time Paul was converted to Christianity and began the missionary journeys which were to take him to various parts of the Empire. Claudius (41–54) came next and was in turn succeeded by Nero (54–68), who became responsible for the first in a series of persecutions against the Christian community. Looking for a scapegoat for an extensive fire in Rome in July 64, which some contemporaries believed might have been instigated by Nero himself to make room for a new city to be built in his honour, the new religious sect of Christianity was seen as a suitable target for blame. Such was the ferocity of the persecution that some Christians were torn to death by dogs while others were used as human torches to light Nero's gardens and paths.

The circumstances describing **St. Paul's** eventual arrival in Rome are narrated in the Acts of the Apostles (chs. 21–28). His preaching in the Holy Land had aroused a good deal of opposition from the local religious leaders, resulting in his arrest by the Romans, probably for his own safety as much as anything else. But at his trial Paul exercised his right as a Roman citizen to appeal to the Emperor. Consequently, he and St. Luke were shipped as prisoners from Caesarea to Rome.

The journey was far from uneventful, particularly when they were shipwrecked off the island of Malta and had to stay there for three months. In due course, however, they sailed from Malta and Paul and his companions put ashore at Puteoli, now Pozzuoli, the port near Naples then serving Rome. On their way into the capital along the Via Appia, they were greeted and offered hospitality by local believers. Acts 28:13–31 deals with Paul's time in the city, where he arrived probably early in AD 61.

It appears that during his two years in Rome, even though he was under some kind of liberal house arrest, he had sufficient freedom to continue his preaching and teaching among both Jewish or Gentile communities. Another suggested possibility, and it can be no more than that, is that Paul was eventually released and then continued with further travels, maybe including Spain, before once again being imprisoned, tried and put to death. Though we would really like to have more definite information about what happened after his arrival in Rome, we just cannot be sure. The only certainty is that the precise details leading up to his death are unknown. Whether it was the culmination of the previous trial or some new accusation against him at a later stage, we can only surmise. According to tradition he was martyred in AD 67, with 29 June being a possible date and as a Roman citizen he was beheaded rather than crucified. On the other hand it could also be possible that he was executed at the end of the two-year period mentioned in the 'Acts'.

However, while we can trace with reasonable accuracy the steps which took St. Paul to Rome, in the case of **St. Peter** it is quite another matter. Having been the dominant leader of the youthful Church growing up in Jerusalem and in Acts 15 the champion of a liberal policy towards Gentiles, there is scant New Testament evidence for his subsequent role in the life of the early Church. Galatians 2:11–14 places him in Antioch with Paul and there is a tradition which claims Peter as its first Bishop. As for his being in Rome, the only possible New Testament reference which locates Peter there is in 1 Peter 5:13 where greetings are sent from 'your sister church in Babylon', taken to be a code name for Rome, though it has to be said that scholars are by no means unanimous as to whether or not Peter wrote the letters ascribed to him.

Nevertheless, there are well-attested early traditions (and tradition must be given its due weight in these matters) which do place him in Rome, e.g. Clement of Rome (c. AD 96), Ignatius (c.107), Irenaeus (c.180). So from quite an early stage it was common knowledge that Peter had worked and died in

Rome, though nothing is known of the length of his stay, and it is also possible that both he and Paul were in Rome at the same time. What is more, by the late 2nd and early 3rd centuries there was a tradition which identified Peter as the first Bishop of Rome, this in turn giving rise to the institution of the Papacy, with subsequent Popes being regarded as successors of Peter.

As for his death and the manner of it, again tradition places this probably in AD 64. Tertullian (212) writes about Peter being crucified and Origen, writing even later in 232, says that he requested to be crucified head downwards. This was because he felt unworthy to be crucified in the same way as his Lord. The suggestion sometimes made that Paul and Peter were executed on the same day in AD 67 is open to question, though it could be possible.

The period of Nero was followed by the Flavian dynasty, Vespasian (69–79), who commissioned the Colosseum, and his two sons, Titus, (79–81) and Domitian (87–96). Whilst on the whole this was a time of relative prosperity and peace within the Empire, for Christians it was under Domitian that the second wave of persecutions was ushered in.

The years 96–180 initiated the era of greatest political stability for Rome since the time of Augustus. It was noted for five Emperors – Nerva (96–98), Trajan (98–117), Hadrian (117–138), Antoninus Pius (138–161) and Marcus Aurelius (161–180). Sometimes referred to as the five good Emperors, this was partly because of the excellence of their rule and partly the way in which they contrasted starkly with Domitian who had preceded them and Commodus who followed them. The fact that this period was known as *The Pax Romana (The Roman Peace)* probably says it all. This was an age when the Empire was at the height of its powers and reached its widest extent. It was characterised by massive building projects, to which Hadrian contributed the Pantheon, as well as all the great engineering works, including the extensive system of aqueducts.

Though Marcus Aurelius, sometimes known as the philosopher-Emperor, did much to champion the poor by founding schools, orphanages and hospitals, as well as trying to humanise criminal laws and the treatment of slaves by their masters, Christians found that he took a somewhat more severe attitude towards them than his three immediate predecessors. Their growing numbers and influence meant that they were regarded with increasing distrust by the imperial authorities and the cultured classes. The result was persecutions in various parts of the Empire.

But if the time of the five good Emperors was the golden age of Rome, with the death of Marcus Aurelius it all came to an end, beginning with his son, Commodus (180–192), who succeeded him. From his time onwards and during most of the third century there was a general decline, with internal dissent, economic collapse and foreign invasions. Christianity, however, continued to flourish and expand throughout the Empire, but in the year 250 the Emperor Decius (249–251) inaugurated the first general persecution of Christians, whereas previously any persecutions had been local and spontaneous.

It was Diocletian (284–305) who set about restoring some order to the Empire, which he did by reforming its government in the face of continuing serious military and economic problems. He divided the Empire into two, east and west, and he himself maintained control over the east. But as far as the Christian community was concerned it was he who, in 303, allowed the last and greatest of all persecutions, sometimes referred to as 'The Great Persecution'. An edict was issued prohibiting Christianity and this led to numerous executions, along with the confiscation of property and the destruction of churches.

Who could have imagined at the height of this persecution that within a decade the situation would have changed dramatically for the Christian community and for the Empire? The agent of the transformation was Constantine (306–337), whose Edict of Milan in 313 allowed freedom of worship for Christians and by the end of his reign Christianity had been adopted as the state religion. At last, after nearly three centuries of sporadic and sometimes intense persecution, Christians were safe. So began a stage in the Empire's history which saw the building of churches, beginning with St. Peter's Basilica in 324, and the establishing by Constantine of a new capital, Byzantium, in 330, which he then renamed Constantinople, modern-day Istanbul. Inevitably this was to lead to the eventual political decline of Rome itself and a significant decrease in its population. Yet, in this western part of the Empire, Rome remained the centre of Christianity and as its secular influence disintegrated so that the Papacy emerged as the sole spiritual and political authority.

The Arch of Constantine

Part 3
ROME
The Pre-Christian Sites

The sites covered in this chapter are those built either before the Christian era or in its early years, but before the conversion of Constantine allowed Christianity to become a respectable and established religion. As will be pointed out more than once during the course of this book, with all that can be seen in Rome the pilgrim visitor may well have to be selective about which particular locations to visit depending on the length of stay. Given the aim to be concise, this chapter can feature only some of the main highlights.

The obvious place to begin the description of the pre-Christian sites is The Forum, which in any city or town was a market place, a meeting point, where people could shop and talk. A typical forum might be surrounded by temples, shops and basilicas, this latter serving their original function as public buildings for various meetings as well as being centres of business and the administration of justice. It was only in Christian times that the word 'Basilica' assumed a religious function.

But in the case of Rome we are talking about more than one Forum. Indeed, there were six Fora in total. The first was the **Roman Forum**, dating back to the time of the Etruscans and Tarquinius Priscus in particular, when in about 600 BC he ordered the draining of the marshland between the Palatine and Capitoline hills (the Cloaca Maxima, the Great Drain mentioned in the last chapter), to prepare the way for the building of the original Forum.

In time, however, this outlived the purposes for which it was built. An ever-increasing population which by the 2nd Century AD had reached more than a million, and the additional requirements therefore placed on such an important area in the city, demanded the building of additional Fora. After all, the Forum was to develop as the centre of the city's commercial, legal and bureaucratic life, not only the heart of Rome but also the heart of the Empire itself. This became the era of the **Imperial Fora**, when the old Republican buildings were restored and rebuilt and the Forum further adorned with new buildings, triumphal arches, columns and statues. The first of these, 54–46 BC, was the work of Julius Caesar after his conquest of Gaul, followed in 31–2 BC by the Forum of Augustus, built to celebrate his victory over the assassins of Caesar – Brutus and Cassius, in 41 BC. Next came the Forum of Vespasian

The Roman Forum

(AD 69–75), then one started by Domitian but completed and dedicated by Nerva (AD 97). But the greatest of all and, indeed, the most ambitious of the Imperial Fora was that of Trajan, (107–113), reputed to cover 25 acres and containing among other structures the huge Basilica Ulpia, the largest in ancient Rome and which can still be seen next to Trajan's Column, which stood between two libraries. The column itself commemorates his victories over the Dacians (approximately modern-day Romania) and is decorated with scenes from these wars. Whereas it used to have a statue of Trajan himself on top, the figure now to be seen is that of St. Peter (since 1587). Note that the remains of these Imperial Fora lie opposite and next to the Roman Forum, with some on the further side of the Via dei Fori Imperiali built by Mussolini.

However, it is the remains of the **Roman** Forum which will most attract your attention. There is a splendid overview of the site from the Capitoline Hill, whether you begin or end your tour here, though there is much to be said for making this your starting-point. Whilst a great deal has been destroyed over the centuries there is still sufficient to give an idea of what the Forum would have been like in its heyday and a strong imagination will enable you to make the most of the layout, some of which is no more than foundations.

Leading the way through the Forum from one end to the other is the Via Sacra, the Sacred Way, which provided an impressive route for triumphal and religious processions. Along this route returning heroes would parade their prisoners and prizes. In the far distance you can glimpse the Colosseum and in front of you and to the right is the Palatine Hill, about which more shortly. On entering the site from the Capitoline you will see the best-preserved monument in this part, the *Arch of Septimius Severus*, built in AD 203 to celebrate his victory over the Parthians. The towering columns adjacent to it on the right are the remains of the *Temple of Saturn*, (5th century BC), focal point for the annual celebration of Saturnalia in December and which also contained the city treasury, while to the left is the reconstruction (1930s) of the *Curia*, the Senate House of ancient Rome, first built by Julius Caesar and later restored. Beyond the Arch of Septimius are the remains of the *Rostra*, a platform which was the tribune from where orations and political speeches were given. Next to the Curia was a large hall, the *Basilica Aemilia*, (originally 179 BC), a meeting place for business and money exchange. Opposite here and to the right of the Rostra are the foundations of the *Basilica Julia*, the law courts dating back to Julius Caesar. Just beyond are three beautiful Corinthian columns from the *Temple of Castor and Phollux*, regarded according to legend as the saviours of Rome when they helped the Republic to victory in 499 BC.

Moving on from here, still on the right, is the remaining part of the circular *Temple of Vesta*, and next to it the *House of the Vestal Virgins*, a rectangular building set around a central garden. Vesta was the goddess of fire, and six virgins selected from noble families were responsible for keeping the sacred flame of Vesta burning in the circular Temple. On the other side of the Forum, across the Via Sacra, is an example of how a temple was transformed into a church – the *Temple of Antoninus and Faustina*, erected in honour of a second-century Emperor and his wife, but later integrated into the church of *San Lorenzo in Miranda*. Further on, still on the same side, is the church of *Santi Cosma e Damiano*, which incorporates the Temple of Romulus. The apse contains a splendid sixth-century mosaic depicting the Second Coming. Next to this are three enormous vaults, all that remains of the *Basilica of Maxentius*, the largest of all the buildings, though it is also called the *Basilica of Constantine* because it was completed and enlarged by him.

Before leaving the Forum, notice the Romanesque bell tower of the church of *Santa Francesca Romana*, which stands like a sentinel over the other churches in the Forum. The public exit is near the *Arch of Titus*, erected in AD 81 to commemorate the role of Titus in the destruction of Jerusalem in AD 70. Fine reliefs under the arch portray the event.

From here it is a short walk up to **The Palatine**, the hill which overlooks the Forum and site of the earliest settlement. Set among pine trees it is a most attractive area and understandably the one where the Emperors built their Imperial Palaces and from which they ruled the Empire. They certainly knew how and where to live! Though much has been destroyed, there is still enough to make a visit most worthwhile. The first to live here after becoming Emperor was Augustus, who, in comparison with some of the later palaces, lived in relatively modest accommodation. The *Domus Augustus* was the public part of his house and the nearby *Domus Livia*, the private part where he lived with his wife, Livia. It is still possible to view many of the wall paintings dating back to this period. Domitian, however, had much more grandiose ideas for the Emperor's residence and at the end of the first century AD created the sumptuous palaces which were to remain the official residence of the Emperor for the next 300 years, the *Domus Augustana*, the private quarters, and the more public *Domus Flavia*. There are also the remains of the *Palace of Septimius Severus*, built by him as an extension of the Domus Augustana, and which also included a bath complex. Along with these you can see the outline of the *Stadium* and the so-called *Huts of Romulus*, believed to be traces of an 8th century BC village. Occupying the highest part of the Palatine are the *Farnese Gardens*, laid out in the 16th century for Cardinal Alessandro Farnese. Beneath these lies a tunnel established by Nero and decorated with stuccoed reliefs. This may have been created to provide a refreshingly cool promenade in the high summer heat or a secret passage between the Palatine and his splendid villa. While exploring the Palatine do take time to utilise some of the vantage points for fine views across the city towards St. Peter's and the *Circus Maximus*, by far the largest and the oldest of Rome's arenas where huge crowds would gather for the chariot-races.

If there is time, or if you can call back on another occasion, the excellent *Palatine Museum* deserves a visit. Having been newly re-organised and refurbished, it exhibits a good collection of Roman sculpture, as well as various artefacts spanning the history of Rome from its origin to the Imperial age and recently discovered mosaics.

Retracing your steps from the Palatine and exiting from the Forum area near the Arch of Titus will bring you to the *Arch of Constantine*, a triple-arched marble construction erected by the senate in AD 315 to celebrate Constantine's victory three years previously over his co-emperor, Maxentius. This was one of the last monuments of Imperial Rome prior to Constantine moving his capital to Byzantium. Most of the stone reliefs were taken from other, older monuments in the city built during the times of Trajan, Hadrian and Marcus Aurelius.

From here it is a short step to **The Colosseum**, possibly the most well-known of Rome's pre-Christian landmarks. How many times have films depicting Imperial Rome contained a mock-up of it, complete with gladiators, prisoners, lions, wild animals, Emperors and blood-thirsty crowds? Fictional though the themes of these films may be, they nevertheless portray only too graphically the gory reality of the Colosseum and the brutal Roman character of that time, though there is some debate as to whether Christians would have been among those who met a cruel death here. Originally commissioned by Vespasian in AD 72, it was inaugurated in AD 80 by Titus. Properly called the

Flavian Amphitheatre it ultimately became known as the Colosseum, probably because of the colossal gilded statue of Nero which stood in front of it. Doric, Ionic and Corinthian half-columns were a distinguishing feature of its outer structure. Capable of holding some 55,000 spectators in its four storeys, seating was according to status and sex. There were four main entrances and once inside 80 arcades provided easy access for the crowds to the staircases which led to the tiered seats. Awnings supported by masts on the upper storey could be erected to shelter spectators from the sun. The Emperor, senators and vestal virgins all occupied special seats in the lower part of the arena.

As you walk around this vast, oval-shaped arena, notice below the main floor the labyrinth of passageways, cages and lifts used for the wild animals. For a particularly impressive overview of the massive interior of the amphitheatre you would be well advised to make your way to the top tiers, either by the stairways or lifts. From up here you can let your imagination run riot as you imagine the packed arena in its heyday. However, with the banning of gladiatorial combat in the 5th century and changing public attitudes, by the 6th century the Colosseum ceased to be a venue for spectator-sports. Though some two-thirds of the original structure has been destroyed over the centuries, much of the stonework being quarried from there to help build other monuments in the city, even today it remains the singularly most impressive memorial symbolising the splendour of Imperial Rome.

The Colosseum

Among the city's pre-Christian sites, few visitors will want to miss the marvellous **Pantheon**, without doubt the best preserved of all Rome's ancient sites. First constructed as a temple by Agrippa in 27-25 BC, what can be seen today, however, is due to Hadrian more than a century later. Erected as a temple to all the gods between AD 118-125, the entrance still preserves the ancient Roman bronze doors. Once inside it is the huge dome which is its most immediately impressive feature. A perfect hemisphere spanning some 43.3 meters with walls 6m thick, it is a supreme achievement of Roman architecture and with its height matching its diameter the whole building is given a sense of harmonious proportion. At the centre of the dome is a 9 m circular hole, the *oculus*, which is the Pantheon's only source of light. In 608 it became a church when the Byzantine Emperor Phocas presented it to Pope Boniface IV, an act which may well have helped to save it for posterity. Indeed, even today it still retains the status of a church. Although much of its ornate decoration has disappeared over the centuries, nevertheless it remains very much as Hadrian planned it. As you walk around this magnificent building, note the tombs of various Italian monarchs and that of the painter Raphael.

Bathing was, of course, an important part of Roman social life and nowhere in the Roman world was complete without a bathing complex and before closing this chapter mention should be made of two such areas. At the foot of the Aventine Hill are the ruins of the gigantic and luxurious **Baths of Caracalla**, completed in AD 217 and able to accommodate 1,600 bathers. A bathe here, however, was no quick dip in a pool! Beginning with a kind of Turkish bath in the *sudatorium*, the bather then moved on to the hot water of the *caldarium*, followed by the opportunity to cool down in the lukewarm water of the *trepidarium* and the cold hall of the *frigidarium*, with a final plunge into the cold water of the swimming pool, the *natatio*. For the wealthy there was the opportunity for a scented rub down to finish off. But a bathing complex like Caracalla provided more than just a facility for washing: art galleries, libraries, gymnasia, shops and gardens were also an integral part of the set-up. As so often seems the case in Rome much of the marble decorations which adorned the complex were later removed, in this case by the Farnese family in the 16th century, to embellish the Palazzo Farnese.

Mention should also be made of the **Baths of Diocletian**, built between AD 298-306 and situated in the Piazza Republica near the main railway station. Even larger than the baths of Caracalla, they could entertain 3,000 bathers. During the 16th century, Michaelangelo converted part of the largest bathing area into the church of *Santa Maria degli Angeli*, adding a splendid new cloister. The area was re-opened to the public in 2000 after restoration.

Part 3
ROME
The Earliest Christian Sites

Just what was life like for Christians in Rome prior to the protection of the state under Constantine? Given the opposition and periodic downright hostility towards them where, for example, did they meet together?

In spite of the popular assumption that the catacombs were the centres for their meetings, it is much more likely that during the first and second centuries these were held in one another's homes, no doubt in the remoter regions of Rome for safety. The owners of these houses were presumably the wealthier members of the Christian community with rooms large enough to hold their fellow-worshippers. To gain some impression of where they gathered, a visit to the church of **San Clemente** is thoroughly recommended. This archaeologically most interesting of buildings is constructed on three levels. The present delightful 12th century church is built over one from the 4th century,

San Clemente

and this in turn over a house which from the end of the first or beginning of the second century is believed to have been used as a *domus ecclesia*, a recognised house for Christian worship, especially in times of persecution.

The upper part of the church has a feeling of perfection about it, with the beautiful marble paving of its floor flanked by ancient columns, which lead the eye upwards to the impressive ceiling and forward to the apse where the superb 12th century mosaic, *The Triumph of the Cross*, is displayed. Decorated with pastoral scenes portraying animals, birds and local peasants, along with other figures of apostles and saints, it has to be the crowning glory of this splendid interior. Notice, too, next to the choir, the spiralling Paschal candlestick decorated with glittering mosaic and also from the 12th century. While still on this level a visit to the Chapel of St. Catherine of Alexandria can be recommended. It is particularly noteworthy for its beautiful 15th century frescoes assigned to Masolino da Panicale, which depict scenes from the saint's life.

However, to make contact with where those earliest Christians met in homes, you need to go down below street-level by stairs which bring you first to the remains of the 4th century basilica. Here are faded Roman frescoes illustrating episodes in the life of St. Clement, the fourth Pope, whom some second-century writers declare to have been a contemporary of Sts. Peter and Paul.

From here it is necessary to descend even further to discover the *domus ecclesia*. The bottom of this particular stairway leads into the ancient Roman level. On one side of a narrow lane are the remains of a second-century Roman apartment block, where some rooms were adapted for the worship of the god Mithras. Mithraism was a religion of Persian origin limited strictly to men and contemporary with Christianity. Still to be seen in the temple are some fine stucco decorations and an altar to the Mithras, showing him slaying a bull.

On the other side of the lane, meanwhile, are the ground-floor rooms of a Roman house, believed to be where early Christians met for Sunday worship. It is a strange feeling to stand in this place which bears so much testimony to the faith and courage of those who lived through times of often intense persecution. Without doubt this is where we are in touch with the earliest of Christian sites in Rome. Indeed, there is much to be said for beginning the visit to San Clemente down here and then working your way up through the levels of history. This most splendid and evocative of churches really should not be missed and ought to be included in every pilgrim itinerary to Rome.

The Catacombs, of course, were another venue for Christian gatherings, but more for burying their dead rather than for holding ordinary religious services or as places of refuge from persecution. It is important to remember that what we now know as 'catacombs' were originally referred to as 'cemeteries'. In the 5th century BC a law was passed forbidding Romans to bury their dead within the city walls. They therefore had to find alternative burial locations on roads leading out of Rome and the famous Via Appia provided a suitably fashionable area for burying the dead. Carved out of the tufa, the soft volcanic rock, there are said to be at least 200 miles of catacombs beneath the city, three of the most significant being along the Appian Way, those of *San Callisto*, *San Sebastiano*, and *Domitilla*.

While there are obviously many pagan tombs, the most famous are the Christians ones, for it was down in the catacombs that they could conduct their ceremonies to bury the dead, presumably including the Eucharist, whilst remaining out of sight of those who wished to persecute them. The body was wrapped in a shroud, laid in a rectangular niche and then enclosed with tiles or marble slabs. The niches, or *loculi*, were usually in tiers. But as well as the individual niches there were larger vaults for families, and by the end of the 3rd century martyrs were also buried here. As a result the catacombs became centres of great devotion. It is in the catacombs, therefore, that we find some of the earliest traces of Christianity in Rome. There are tombs, for example, with paintings going back to the 2nd century and illustrating the faith of the people. Also to be seen are paintings of Peter and Paul as well as the Christian monogram, the *chi-rho*, made from the first two Greek letters of Christ's name.

The Catacombs of *San Callisto*, who became Pope in 217, are probably the most frequently visited, which means that at busy times you may have to wait your turn to be shown around, especially if you are part of a group. But it is worth the wait. There are four levels of extensive underground galleries lined with niches and vaults, many with very simple inscriptions while others, the most important crypts, are decorated with paintings. Some portray the symbols of the fish or the sacrificial lamb or various New Testament scenes. One such crypt contains the tombs of a number of the early Popes and another, the crypt of St. Cecilia, the patron saint of music, once contained her body before it was transferred to the church which now bears her name, the church of St. Cecilia in Trastevere. It is believed that the relics of Peter and Paul may have been hidden in the nearby *Catacombs of San Sebastiano* during a period of persecution in the third century. These, too, are well worth a visit as an alternative to those of San Callisto.

But, of course, things were to change dramatically for the Christian population under the Emperor Constantine. In 312, at the battle of Milvian Bridge, just north of Rome, it is said that Constantine saw in the sky a vision of a flaming Cross bearing the words, 'by this sign you shall conquer', though there is a suggestion that it was only on his death-bed that he finally converted. The following year he issued the Edict of Milan, which granted tolerance throughout the Empire to the Christian religion and later on in his reign Christianity became established as the state religion. It was from this period onwards that the Cross became acknowledged as the Christian symbol of victory, rather than as previously – a symbol of punishment, and the Cross could now be used openly in Rome to indicate centres of Christian worship. It was also during Constantine's reign that the building of great Basilicas began, but more about these in subsequent chapters.

Part 4
PAULINE AND PETRINE SITES

You will no doubt appreciate that when discussing ancient sites reputedly associated with notable historical figures, there tends to be a liberal use of words like, 'maybe', 'possibly', 'perhaps', because precise pinpointing of particular sites is not always easy. Many locations are based on historical traditions and these are not lightly to be dismissed. But a helpful dose of humility, rather than being too dogmatic, is sometimes useful in these situations! Also, while there are specific sites identifiable with each Apostle, there are also those which may be common to both.

ST. PAUL

The Porta San Paolo is said to be the gate through which he was led to execution. This, however, was a later naming of the gate in honour of the Apostle because the Aurelian Wall in which it is set was not begun until AD 270. Previously called the *Porta Ostiense*, St. Paul's Gate is set in one of the best-preserved sections of the Wall, which was built by the Emperor Marcus Aurelius as protection for the city. The part of the gate facing the city is original Aurelian, and the twin defensive towers on the other side date back to the 6th century AD.

Close by the gate is the *Pyramid of Gaius Cestius*, built as his tomb in 12 BC and probably one the last things seen by Paul on his way to execution. Also near here and inside the walls is the lovely *Protestant Cemetery* containing the graves of Keats and Shelley.

From St. Paul's Gate, the Via Ostiense leads to the Basilica of **San Paulo fuori le Mura**, *St. Paul Without the Walls*. This was one of three great basilicas erected during the time of Constantine, the others being St. Peter's and San Giovanni in Laterano. San Paolo was built by the Emperor in AD 324 to commemorate the execution and martyrdom of the Apostle at nearby Tre Fontane. Following the lines of the original basilica, the current building dates from 1854 when the church had to be reconstructed following a fire in 1823.

The entrance faces the Tiber and is reached through a large courtyard with a towering marble statue of St. Paul. Surviving features from the previous

St Paul Outside the Walls

church are bronze doors inlaid with silver, made in Constantinople and dating back to 1070; a 12th century Paschal candlestick; the splendid 13th century marble canopy above the high altar; and, of course, the magnificent cloisters. On entering the basilica it is difficult not to be impressed by its vastness, with double aisles on either side separated by 80 granite columns. As you walk around, observe the mosaic portraits of all the Popes from St. Peter onwards, some of them surviving the fire of the previous church. There are also very fine mosaics in the apse of Christ with St. Peter, St. Paul, St. Andrew and St. Luke.

Reference has already been made to the impressive canopy over the high altar and set within the Triumphal Arch, which is itself decorated with beautiful restored mosaics from the 5th century. Beneath the altar is the *confessio* where the body of St. Paul is believed to have been buried. Over the tomb is a marble slab which bears the name of the Apostle.

To the left of the apse is the only chapel to have survived the fire. This is where St. Ignatius and his followers took the vows which instituted the Jesuits as a religious order. Notice the very fine 13th century crucifix.

The cloisters to the right of the building are not to be missed as they are one of the most beautiful in Rome. Completed in the early 13th century they amazingly escaped the holocaust six centuries later. The colourful columns, some twisting and others straight, some carved out of marble and others inlaid with gold, are a fine example of the Roman school of mosaic art introduced in the 11th century by the Cosmati family. No visits to St. Paul's can be regarded as complete without taking time to wander round the cloisters and soak up their atmosphere.

If this imposing basilica was built over the cemetery containing St. Paul's tomb, then according to tradition it was not far from here, at **Tre Fontane**, that his execution took place. As a Roman citizen Paul was entitled to the relatively swift form of execution by beheading rather than the drawn-out process of crucifixion. The tradition is that having been decapitated, his head bounced three times and at these spots three springs burst forth. This is now the Trappist Monastery of Tre Fontane. In this delightful escape from the hurly-burly of city life the most distracting noises are the singing of birds and the gurgling of water. A walk through the grounds of this leafy haven brings you to the church of *San Paulo alle Tre Fontane*, one of three churches to be found here and built in the 5th century over what was believed to be the scene of the Apostle's execution. Apart from a column in one corner to which St. Paul is said to have been bound, there are now no traces of the original church, the current one dating back to 1599 when it was rebuilt by Giacomo della Porta.

These, then, are the three main sites associated particularly with St. Paul. However, there are 'ifs', 'maybes' and 'possibles' about a further location. This is the **Mamertine Prison**, often associated by tradition with the imprisonment of St. Peter, nevertheless, if Peter and Paul *were* imprisoned together and executed on the same day, then Paul may also have been held captive here. A dark, dank underground dungeon, those prisoners who were not executed down here often died from starvation, the bodies being thrown into the adjacent Cloaca Maxima, Rome's main sewer. Legend says that Peter (and maybe Paul) caused a miraculous spring to well up in the prison, the water from which was used to baptise the prison guards who were converted to Christianity.

One further 'maybe' is the church of *San Giovanni in Laterano*, about which more later, in that the reliquaries by the Papal Altar were believed to contain the heads of both Apostles.

ST. PETER

Having ended the section on the Pauline sites with two that may have been associated with both Apostles, it therefore seems appropriate to begin this section on St. Peter in Rome with another site that may have been common to them both – the Appian Way. Brief reference has already been made to this in connection with the catacombs and the possibility that the bodies of Peter and Paul may have been accommodated for a time in the catacombs of San Sebastian.

Not to be confused with the new Appian Way, the Via Appia Antica was begun in 312 BC and became a main road from the city stretching initially to near Naples and then later, when extended in 190 BC, to Brindisi. Originally known as the Queen of Roads, it was very straight and surfaced with huge blocks of volcanic stone, a route along which Romans built their villas and created their cemeteries as well as providing a most important commercial access to the city.

Today, lined with cypresses, churches, tombs and catacombs, the first part of this road is rich in early Christian associations. It would have been along here that Paul was brought into the city as a prisoner after landing at Puteoli, (Acts 28:13–14). As far as Peter is concerned, there is a story that while fleeing from Rome to avoid martyrdom Christ is said to have appeared to him on the Appian Way. 'Domine, quo vadis?' asked Peter, ('Lord, where are you going?') and received the reply, 'Venio iterum crucifigi' ('I come to be crucified a second time'). This response so shamed Peter that he returned to Rome and his eventual crucifixion. On the left leaving the city, the delightful little chapel of *Domine Quo Vadis?* marks the spot of this reputed encounter. Inside, the stone supposed to be marked with the footprints of Christ is a replica of the original in the church of San Sebastiano.

Back in the city itself, apart from St. Peter's Basilica, which will be dealt with in connection with the Vatican, is the church of *San Pietro in Vincoli*, St. Peter in Chains. Dating back to the early 5th century, the church was subsequently rebuilt in the 8th and 15th centuries. Of the various Petrine sites in Rome, the chains are probably the most venerated. Now kept in a reliquary under the high altar they are said to be both the chains with which Peter was bound while imprisoned in the Mamertine Prison and those which shackled him in Jerusalem, both sets of chains having been miraculously fused together. Their initial fame was no doubt helped by the fact that they were mentioned at the Council of Ephesus in AD 431.

The tomb of Pope Julius II, who apparently had grandiose ideas about his final resting place, is the other significant feature of the church. His plan was for a much larger tabernacle with 40 statues, all to be the work of Michelangelo, but matters did not work out that way. Most of what can now be seen was the product of the artist's students, with the exception of his masterpiece, *Moses*. Sculptured probably between 1514-16 out of a single piece of marble, it is a magnificent representation of the power and strength of prophetic character. Set between sculptures of Leah and Rachel, the imposing *Moses* totally dominates the tomb of the proud Julius.

But of course, the greatest of all churches associated with St. Peter is that which takes his own name as part of the Vatican City, *St. Peter's Basilica*, and this will be dealt with in the next chapter.

The Mamertine prison – Altar and Spring   © *Sacred Destinations Images*

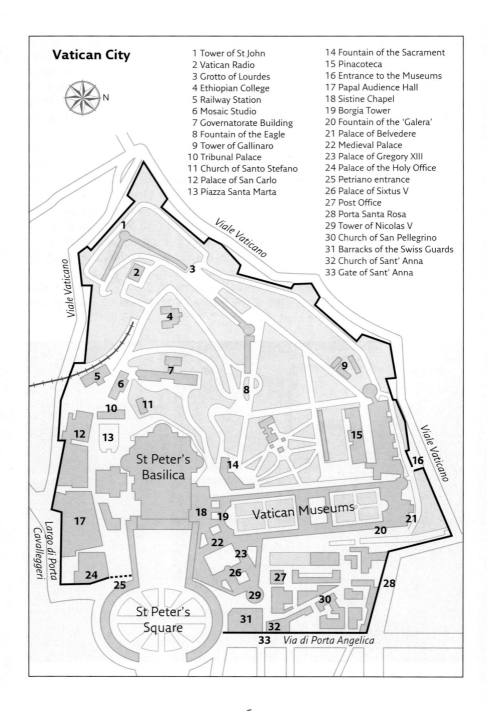

Vatican City

N

1 Tower of St John
2 Vatican Radio
3 Grotto of Lourdes
4 Ethiopian College
5 Railway Station
6 Mosaic Studio
7 Governatorate Building
8 Fountain of the Eagle
9 Tower of Gallinaro
10 Tribunal Palace
11 Church of Santo Stefano
12 Palace of San Carlo
13 Piazza Santa Marta

14 Fountain of the Sacrament
15 Pinacoteca
16 Entrance to the Museums
17 Papal Audience Hall
18 Sistine Chapel
19 Borgia Tower
20 Fountain of the 'Galera'
21 Palace of Belvedere
22 Medieval Palace
23 Palace of Gregory XIII
24 Palace of the Holy Office
25 Petriano entrance
26 Palace of Sixtus V
27 Post Office
28 Porta Santa Rosa
29 Tower of Nicolas V
30 Church of San Pellegrino
31 Barracks of the Swiss Guards
32 Church of Sant' Anna
33 Gate of Sant' Anna

Viale Vaticano

Viale Vaticano

Viale Vaticano

St Peter's
Basilica

Vatican Museums

Largo di Porta
Cavalleggeri

St Peter's
Square

Via di Porta Angelica

Part 6
THE VATICAN

Established on 11th February 1929, the Vatican City is a sovereign state under the Pope's authority. It has its own currency, postal and telephone services, along with its own newspaper, Radio and TV stations, shops and banks. Situated west of the Tiber it is set within 40 ft high walls built in the 9th century by Pope Leo IV as protection against invaders. Within the comparatively small area of 106 acres are the Vatican and its gardens, the Museum and Sistine Chapel, St. Peter's Basilica and St. Peter's Square. Over all this the Pope has legislative, executive and judicial powers. Italy recognises the Vatican City as his exclusive territory and acknowledges his sovereignty in international relations.

The Pope's own apartments are in a corner of the Vatican Palace and overlook St. Peter's Square. His own personal bodyguard is the Swiss Guard, established in the early 16th century by Pope Julius II. Distinctive in their yellow, red and blue stripes, they perform not only a ceremonial role but also a security one. Made up of young, unmarried Swiss Roman Catholics, they must serve a minimum of two years.

Standing like a sentinel guarding the Vatican City is the magnificent **St. Peter's Basilica**, whose massive dome dominates so much of the Rome skyline. The Emperor Constantine originally began the church in AD 324 over the tomb of St. Peter and not far from where he was martyred in the Circus of Nero. A lofty building rather in the style of St. Paul Without the Walls, it was richly decorated with mosaics. While subsequent centuries saw various enlargements, they also witnessed its falling into disrepair and it was not until Pope Julius II, he of the very grand ideas, that a new building was begun in 1506. But having laid the foundation stone in that year Julius was never to see the completion of his enterprise, for the work took more than a century and the new St. Peter's was only finally consecrated in 1626. During this period various great Renaissance and Baroque artists contributed their skills, among them Raphael, Michelangelo and Bernini.

As you face the main entrance to the basilica you will see five sets of bronze doors beneath the pillared portico. The one on the extreme right is *the Holy Door*, opened only by the Pope in Holy Years. The portico houses one of the great treasures of the original church, Giotto's mosaic of Christ walking on the water and dating back to about 1298, though it is now very faded and difficult to see.

Once inside there is an impressive sense of vastness, partly due to the fact that everyone in the building seems to be totally dwarfed by the hugeness of the structure. Indeed, marks on the floor indicate that St. Peter's is larger than either St. Paul's, London or Notre-Dame, Paris, among others that don't quite measure up in terms of length! Standing here and looking straight ahead down the nave, the first thing which strikes is Bernini's massive and much-celebrated bronze *baldacchino* or *canopy* over the Papal altar, from where only the Pope can celebrate Mass. Commissioned in 1624 by Pope Urban VIII but not completed until 1633, it is more than 60 feet high and as tall as the Palazzo Farnese. Much of the bronze out of which it is constructed is thought to have been taken from the Pantheon.

Before moving on down through the nave, turn right to view one of Michelangelo's great gems, the *Pieta*. Now protected by a glass screen after being damaged by a vandal in 1972 and then skilfully restored the following year, Michelangelo created it in 1499 when he was only 25 and it was hailed as a masterpiece. The most famous piece of art in the whole building, it is the only sculpture that the artist ever signed. Carved from a single piece of marble it is a life-size and very sensitive presentation of a youthful Mary cradling the dead body of Christ in her arms.

Walking down the right aisle you pass a number of chapels until you come eventually to the majestic bronze *Statue of St. Peter*, the dating of which has been a matter of some debate. Some state it to be from the 5th century and others from the 13th – it is probably more likely to be the latter. Look carefully and you will see how the right foot of the Apostle has been worn smooth from the touch of countless pilgrims over the centuries.

This brings you back to the Papal Altar under which is reputedly the *Tomb of St. Peter*. It was during the Second World War that workmen discovered beneath the basilica an ancient cemetery from before the time of Constantine containing pagan and Christian tombs, and in particular the tomb supposed to be that of St. Peter. A stairway near the Altar leads down to the crypt where there are also the tombs of some of Peter's Papal successors.

Above the altar and its canopy is the enormous *Dome*, some 450ft above ground level and designed by Michelangelo, though the building of it was completed only after his death. Running round the interior of the dome in letters more than 6ft high are the words: 'Tu es Petrus et super hanc petram aedidicabo ecclesiam meam et tibi dabo claves regni caelorum' ('You are Peter, and on this rock I will build my church ...... And I will give you the keys of the kingdom of heaven' – Matthew 16:18–19). It is possible to ascend the dome from outside St. Peter's, either by hundreds of steps or by lift. High up from the

St Peter's

Within St Peter's

outside provides magnificent views of the Vatican gardens and over St. Peter's Square, whilst from the first gallery inside the dome the awesome scale of the basilica is stunningly apparent.

While still inside the building at ground level, behind the altar and in the apse at the far end, is Bernini's *Throne of St. Peter*. Made from bronze, this encloses an ancient wood and ivory chair once believed to be the chair from which St. Peter delivered his first sermon to the Romans. Its dating, however, goes back only to the 9th century.

The above has merely sketched out the more obvious and most important things to be seen in this greatest of all basilicas. With its numerous chapels, altars and works of art, there is so much more to be seen, but how long you can spend in here exploring the various details will depend on other elements of your itinerary for the day. All too often time is of the essence, but time is something which St. Peter's amply repays.

To the right of the basilica is the Vatican Palace, home to the **Vatican Museums** and it is through these that you have access to the Sistine Chapel. To visit all the Museums would be a most daunting undertaking, both physically and mentally! From the entrance there are four colour-coded, one-way routes, the shortest being about 90 minutes and the longest 5 hours, though you could probably do a quick dash through if the Sistine Chapel is your only interest.

Begun during the time of Pope Julius II, the galleries house one of the world's most important collections of art, with wonderful Greek and Roman antiquities, along with paintings by some of Italy's finest artists, such as Raphael, Michelangelo and Leonardo da Vinci. Again, the requirements of this book mean it is possible only to indicate some of the main highlights.

One of the first displays you come to on the lower floor is the collection of *Egyptian and Assyrian Art*, containing Egyptian sculptures found mainly in and around Rome, a good deal of which was brought back to Rome from Egypt in Imperial times. There are also mummies and mummy cases. Adjoining this is the *Pio-Clementine Museum*, with a display of the Vatican's finest Classical statues, one of the most splendid being the *Belvedere Apollo*, a Roman marble copy of a 4th century Greek bronze, and situated in the octagonal Belvedere Courtyard. Going upstairs from here brings you to the *Etruscan Museum* exhibiting Greek, Roman and Etruscan art in the form of sarcophagi, ornaments, statues and a collection of outstanding Greek vases. Passing through a gallery lined with Roman statues and adorned with candelabra leads to a corridor lined with beautiful floor to ceiling Flemish tapestries by Pieter van Aelst from cartoons by Raphael. This in turn passes into the *Gallery of Maps*, with maps and views of regions and towns in Italy painted on the walls (1580–1583). Also on this upper level are the *Raphael Rooms*, four rooms painted by Raphael and his pupils (1508–1525) for the private apartments of Pope Julius II, and these are certainly worth a viewing if time permits.

Down from this level is the **Sistine Chapel**, named after the Pope for whom it was built, Sixtus IV, during the latter part of the 15th century. It was to become the Papal domestic chapel and, of course, the meeting-place for the Conclave of Cardinals which elects a new Pope. But its main claim to fame lies in the magnificent frescoes that cover the walls and ceiling.

When you first enter the Chapel at the altar end it can seem extremely daunting, both because of the many other people who are also there and the overwhelming impact of the paintings themselves. The temptation is to start looking at the ceiling and the altar wall as soon as you enter, but this is not the best way to view them. Keeping your eyes firmly fixed in front of you, work your way through the other people and head towards the far wall which is the entrance wall. When you come to the screen across the Chapel, about three-quarters of the way down, turn round and look back towards the altar. Then you will see the ceiling and the altar wall in their proper perspectives.

The first paintings were those on the side walls, created by the finest Florentine and Umbrian artists of the late 15th and early 16th centuries, among whom was Botticelli. Though it is the subsequent work of Michelangelo which tends to claim the visitor's attention, these wall paintings in the Chapel should not be overlooked.

As you face the altar wall and starting from that end, the six frescoes on the left hand wall depict scenes from the life of Moses.

1. *The Journey of Moses to Egypt*
This one picture also portrays the farewell to his father-in-law, Jethro, Moses' return to Egypt with his family, and the Circumcision of his second-born child.

2. *Events in the Life of Moses*
Here you can see the killing of the Egyptian, the struggle with the shepherds to defend Jethro's daughter, and the incident of the Burning Bush.

3. *The Crossing of the Red Sea*

4. *The Tablets of the Law*
Notice also the representation of Moses climbing Mount Sinai, the worship of the golden calf and the punishment of the idolatrous Jews.

5. *The Punishment of Korah, Dathan and Abiram*
These were the Jewish priests who denied Moses and Aaron authority over the people.

6. *The Legacy and Death of Moses*
The final panel is on the entrance wall and its theme is *The Dispute over the Body of Moses.*

The six frescoes on the right hand wall, again beginning from the altar end, describe selected scenes from the ministry of Christ

1. *The Baptism of Christ*

2. *The Temptation of Christ*
This panel also includes a painting of the Cleansing of the Leper.

3. *The Calling of the First Disciples*
Peter and Andrew occupy the foreground, with James and John in the background.

4. *The Sermon on the Mount*
This, too, is coupled with one of Christ's miracles – the Curing of the Leper.

5. *The Charge to Peter*
Here you can see the handing over of the Keys to Peter, alongside a portrayal of the payment of tribute and the attempted stoning of Christ.

6. *The Last Supper*
If you look carefully, there is a window in which three episodes from the Passion of Christ are presented – the Garden of Gethsemane, the Arrest of Jesus and the Crucifixion.

In The Vatican Museum

As with the Moses sequence, the final episode here, *The Resurrection*, is again on the entrance wall.

In 1508 Michelangelo received a summons from Julius II to paint the Chapel's *Ceiling*. This, of course, was a considerable challenge to someone who up until then was primarily a sculptor without any experience of painting frescoes. His bitterly jealous rival, Bramante, is said to have instigated the idea with Julius in the hope that Michelangelo would either refuse or, if he accepted, prove to be a dismal failure. Initially he was minded to decline such a monumental commission. However, pressurised by the Pope, he gave in and the rest, as they say, is history.

The next four years, until 1512, Michelangelo was to spend in highly uncomfortable positions on scaffolding that he himself designed for this particular task. His original intention was to employ assistants, but discovering them to be an incompetent lot he sacked them all! Beginning from the altar end the first three main central panels of the ceiling depict the story of Creation, with a powerful but terrifying God dividing Light from Darkness, Creating the sun, moon and planets, and Separating the Land from the Sea. The theme of the next three panels is about the creation of human beings, the Creation of Adam, the Creation of Eve, and Original Sin and the banishment from the garden. The final three panels deal with the Fall and the subsequent re-birth of creation – the Sacrifice of Noah, the Flood, the Drunkenness of Noah.

Around the main panels are painted the figures of seven Old Testament Prophets (Jonah, Jeremiah, Daniel, Ezekiel, Isaiah, Joel and Zechariah) and five Classical Sybils. During all this time Julius constantly chivvied Michelangelo until this great masterpiece was finished – a truly remarkable achievement by one person. No one who has not visited the Sistine Chapel can begin to imagine what this one artist accomplished.

If, having completed the ceiling, Michelangelo thought that he had more than done his bit for Julius and the Chapel, then more than twenty years later, in 1534, he was to realise just how wrong he was! No sooner had Paul III become Pope than Michelangelo was commissioned to paint the altar wall fresco, the *'Last Judgement'*, another masterpiece which was to take a further seven years out of his life. Set around the powerful and ferociously stern figure of Christ as Judge, the painting portrays an atmosphere of doom as the souls of the dead are brought to face their judgement. It is very much a *'dies irae'*, a day of wrath depiction. There is little tenderness in it apart from the figure of the Virgin Mary. Something of Michelangelo's own spiritual crisis is depicted in the fresco and, indeed, his own tormented face is painted on the wrinkled human skin held by St. Batholomew. Though Paul III acknowledged the greatness of the painting some of his successors were much less appreciative, with Paul IV objecting to so much nudity that loincloths or breeches had to be painted over some of the figures. One Pope even wanted the whole wall whitewashed over!

Beginning in 1979 and completed in 1994, a major restoration of the frescoes was undertaken. Indeed, the restoration took longer than the original painting of them! Financed by a Japanese television company, the team of experts was able to separate Michelangelo's original work from that of his later restorers and this revealed a rich vibrancy of colour as compared with the previously seen more muted colours. They also removed the additional clothing on some of the figures as required by Paul IV and others. But, as with the original, so the restoration also produced a good deal of controversy with some experts claiming that the restorers had destroyed Michelangelo's work by producing such vibrant colours. However, what we now see is much more likely to be what the great artist intended.

There is, of course, a good deal more to be seen in the Vatican museums, including the *Pinacoteca (picture gallery)*, with its marvellous collection of medieval, Renaissance and baroque art, with masterpieces by Caravaggio, Giotto and Leonardo da Vinci among many others. Much, however, will depend on the provisions of your particular itinerary as to whether or not a viewing of the gallery is possible. What has been outlined above may be all that you really have time for.

PAPAL AUDIENCES

These are usually held on Wednesday mornings at 11 a.m., sometimes in the Basilica or the Hall of Papal Audiences. During the summer they are usually held in St. Peter's Square or at Castel Gondolfo when the Pope is resident there. Tickets are free but must be reserved and can be obtained from the Office of the Prefettura della Casa Pontificia, which is usually open from Mon–Sat, 9.00 a.m.–1 p.m. The office can be found through the bronze door at the end of the colonnade on the right side of the piazza. It is also possible to write in advance to:

Prefettura della Casa Pontificia,
00120 Citta del Vaticano,
Italy.

Telephone: 06 – 6988 3273

Part 7
ROME
Churches and Museums

How much you can see in any one visit to Rome is largely determined either by your organised itinerary or by whatever free time you may have to explore on your own, as well, of course, as your own personal interest and inclinations. This chapter highlights some of the other churches not already mentioned and which amply repay visiting if time permits, along with some of the notable museums.

Beginning, then, with churches, **San Giovanni in Laterano** (Piazza di San Giovanni in Laterano) is a strong candidate for a visit as it is one of the three Constantinian churches in Rome, plus the fact that along with St. Peter's, Santa Maria Maggiore and San Paolo Fuori le Mura, it is one of the four Patriarchal Basilicas. Built around 313 it was the first Christian basilica and as the Pope is also the Bishop of Rome and because the church contained the *cathedra*, or bishop's chair, it became the city's Cathedral. It retains that distinction even today for on Holy Thursday this is where the Pope celebrates Mass. From the 4th century until 1309 when the papacy moved to Avignon, San Giovanni was the home of the Pope and during that period was accorded the significance of the Vatican today. Indeed, until the 19th century, the Popes were crowned here.

Though much rebuilt over the centuries it still retains its original basilica style. The interior was re-styled in 1646 and the façade added in the 1730s. The enormous central bronze doors of the main entrance were originally from the Senate House in the Roman Forum and the closed door to the far right is opened only during Holy Years. Once inside, the particularly noteworthy features are: the octagonal *Baptistry* – the original dates back to Constantine, and though it has been much restored there are some beautiful 5th century mosaics to be seen; the Papal altar, with the Gothic *baldacchino* decorated with 14th century frescoes; the two busts of Sts. Peter and Paul, which were once believed to contain their heads; and the fragment of a fresco attributed to Giotto in which Pope Boniface VIII is depicted announcing the first Holy Year in 1300. Also a 'must' are *the Cloisters*, dating back to the 13th century and generally agreed to be the most beautiful of their kind in Rome, with their twisted columns and inlaid marble mosaics.

The adjacent *Lateran Palace* was the official residence of the Pope until 1309, and after the massive fire of 1309 which destroyed both the basilica and the palace, it remained in ruins until it was rebuilt in 1586. One important survivor of the fire was the *Scala Santa*, now located opposite the palace. Traditionally these 28 steps are regarded as those by which Christ ascended to Pontius Pilate's palace in Jerusalem and are said to have been brought to Rome by St. Helena. Leading up to the Sancta Sanctorum or Chapel of San Lorenzo, which was the Pope's private chapel in the old palace, the faithful climb them only on their knees. Though the stairs themselves are marble they are now encased in wood for protection.

Santa Croce in Gerusalemme (Piazza di Santa Croce in Gerusalemme) also owes much to the mother of Constantine. It is believed to be situated on the remains of a palace which for a time was Helena's home, a hall of which was transformed into Santa Croce some time during the first half of the fourth century, though it was rebuilt and extended in both the 12th and 18th centuries. Tradition states that in Jerusalem Helena discovered fragments of the True Cross and a nail, as well as two thorns from Christ's crown, a piece of wood from the cross of the penitent thief, and the actual finger which St. Thomas placed in Christ's wounded side. She is said to have brought these back to Rome about 320, and subsequently the church was built to house the relics. These are now located behind glass in a chapel off the left aisle. Steps from the right aisle lead down to the delightful Chapel of St. Helen, whose mosaics were created in the 5th century but redesigned in 1484.

Santa Maria Maggiore (Piazza di Santa Maria Maggiore) can claim with some justification to be the grandest of the many churches in Rome dedicated to Mary. Ranking fourth among the great patriarchal basilicas of Rome, it is one of those masterpieces about which you begin to run out of superlatives. Part of the splendour of this church is the way in which various architectural styles blend agreeably together. Though the façade and the two cupolas are 18th century, once you enter the church you are confronted with a most majestic structure in which the original magnificent nave and columns all belong to the 5th century. The thirty-six mosaics above the columns also come from the 5th century and show scenes from the Old Testament, and those on the triumphal arch are also from that period. The wonderful mosaics in the apse date from the 13th century, portraying Mary as a Byzantine empress being crowned by Christ as the Queen of Heaven. The striking floor is 12th century, and yet, for all the variety of styles, there is an overwhelming sense of harmony.

In the 16th and 17th century two chapels were added to the basilica. To the right of the altar is the opulent *Sistine Chapel*, built for Pope Sixtus V (1584–7) and covered in marble looted from ancient Roman buildings. On the opposite side of the altar is the *Pauline Chapel*, completed in 1611 for Pope Paul V and which some may consider over-decorated. It was designed by Flaminio Ponzio, architect of the Villa Borghese, to house in its altar the famous icon of the 'Madonna and Child', dated by some to the 9th century and others to the 12th/13th. Both Popes are buried in their respective chapels. It is from the dome of the Pauline Chapel that on the 5th August each year, during Mass, thousands of white petals are released to commemorate the legend of the snowfall on 5th August 352 which led to the building of the basilica.

Nearest the door on the left side of the nave is the beautiful *Sforza Chapel*, named after Cardinal Guido Ascanio Sforza. Whereas previously it was believed that Michelangelo may have entrusted the commission for this chapel to an assistant, more recently recovered documents indicate that not only did the great artist design it, but also that he personally supervised every detail of the work from its beginning in 1562 until his death in 1564. Dedicated to the Assumption, recent renovation has now restored the chapel to its former glory.

Other churches dedicated to Mary and which are well worth a visit are: **Santa Maria del Popolo** (Piazza del Popolo), one of the first Renaissance churches in Rome and a treasure trove of artistic splendour, including masterpieces by Caravaggio, the *Conversion of St. Paul* and the *Crucifixion of St. Peter*, as well as the Chigi chapel, begun by Raphael and completed by Bernini; **Santa Maria in Trastevere** (Piazza Santa Maria in Trastevere), probably the site of the oldest church in Rome and its first official place of worship, dating back to the 4th century, and certainly one of the first to be dedicated to Mary. The present building, however, is dated back to the 12th century and contains some very fine mosaics from the 12th-13th centuries; **Santa Maria in Cosmedin** (Piazza della Bocca della Verita), built originally in the 6th century and subsequently much restored, particularly in the 12th century, is a most beautiful church containing many fine examples of Cosmati decorations in marble and colourful mosaics, most notably the mosaic nave floor, the choir, the bishop's throne, and the 13th century *baldacchino* over the main altar.

So the list of churches could go on and the compilers of pilgrim itineraries obviously need to be selective and choose those churches which they deem to be of special interest to their particular groups. Similarly the individual visitor will need to be equally choosy, depending on personal preferences, given everything else in this city which demands to be visited. One thing is certain: if Rome wasn't built in a day, its many churches certainly can't be visited in a day!

As for the **museums**, the most significant, the Vatican Museum, has already been described (see pages 31–35). Mind you, even that Museum is not the sole repository of Rome's past artistic glories. Set in the Villa Borghese, the **Museo and Galleria Borghese** (Piazzale Scipione Borghese 5) contains one of the finest private art and sculpture collections anywhere in the world. In the early 17th century Cardinal Scipione Borghese, who was part of the noble and wealthy Borghese family, began creating a huge and magnificent park in the city. Over the years the park was variously enlarged and redesigned by the family, and at the beginning of the 20th century it was taken into State ownership. Within the gardens the pleasure-loving Cardinal, who clearly had an eye for the artistic masterpiece, had a Villa specially built to display his remarkable paintings and sculptures.

The sculptures can be seen on the ground floor in the *Museo*. Although some 200 pieces of sculpture were sold in the early 19th century to the Louvre in Paris, the remaining pieces are still extremely worthy of a viewing, for they include some of Bernini's finest and, indeed, earliest works, including *Apollo and Daphne*, and *David*, the latter's face believed to be modelled on Bernini's own. There is also a statue of *Venus*, posed for by the sister of Napoleon, Pauline Borghese. On display, too, are some fine Roman copies of Greek originals. The upper floor, the *Galleria*, exhibits superlative Baroque and Renaissance paintings by artists such as Botticelli, Caravaggio, Raphael, Rubens, Titian and Veronese – a veritable treasure-trove for the art lover!

Situated on the Piazza del Campidoglio are the recently renovated and refurbished **Capitoline Museums**. The piazza, designed originally by Michelangelo in the 1530s for Pope Paul III and later completed by others, is best approached by the stairway, also by Michelangelo, leading up from the Via del Teatro di Marcello. At the top and straight ahead is Rome's civic centre, the Palazzo Senatorio. However, to the left is the Palazzo Nuovo and to the right the Palazzo dei Conservatori, and these two together form the Capitoline Museums, one of the oldest public museums in the world and home to some of Rome's finest works of art. In the centre of the piazza you will notice the magnificent equestrian statue of the Emperor Marcus Aurelius, though this is but a copy, and an excellent one at that, of the original which was re-located here by Michelangelo to be the centrepiece of his new piazza. The statue was removed for renovation in the late 20th century.

It all began in 1471 when Pope Sixtus IV presented a group of sculptures to the city. Today paintings as well as sculptures are exhibited in the museums. The main entrance is through the *Palazzo dei Conservatori*, whose courtyard displays fragments of a huge statue of Constantine found in the Forum. On the first floor are fine sculptures, including one by Bernini of his patron *Urban VIII* and the famous *She-Wolf* suckling Romulus and Remus. Though the wolf is a 5th century BC Etruscan bronze, the twins were not added until the 15th century. The second floor hosts the art galleries which contain several significant works, the most outstanding of which is Caravaggio's *St. John the Baptist*, a very unorthodox and sensual portrayal of the saint. In addition, it would be inexcusable to overlook the other paintings by such as Tintoretto, Titian, Van Dyck and Veronese.

A passageway beneath the Piazza del Campidoglio leads to the *Palazzo Nuovo*. Here are some exceptional examples of Greek and Roman sculpture, including portrait busts of emperors, philosophers and poets, along with a very sensitive 3rd century BC statue of a dying Gaul and the sensuous *Capitoline Venus*.

Towards the end of 2005 a new glass-covered and climate-controlled wing to the museum was opened containing, among other items, the recently unearthed remains of the oldest stone building in Rome, the Temple of Jupiter, including a 22 foot stretch of temple wall. Dedicated to the gods Jupiter, Juno and Minerva, the Temple was dedicated in 509 BC and was the focal point of both religion and politics, as well as the site of triumphal military processions. In its heyday the statues of the gods, the doors and the roof were sumptuously adorned with gleaming gold. Also back on display is the restored original bronze equestrian statue of Marcus Aurelius referred to above, probably the most illustrious statue of the Ancient world, and a gigantic head of the Emperor Constantine.

A further possibility, though tickets have to be booked in advance, is the Golden House, **Domus Aurea**, (Viale della Domus Aurea), built by Nero in AD 64 after the great fire which destroyed some two-thirds of Rome. Set in a vast landscaped park with vineyards and an artificial lake, the palace was Nero at his most shamelessly extravagant. The whole of the façade was gilded, and rooms, halls and corridors were decorated with gold, silver and precious stones. Near the entrance stood a gigantic gilt bronze statue of Nero, the Colossus, built in imitation of the Colossus of Rhodes. But after Nero's death in AD 68 every effort was made to expunge his memory and to eliminate all traces of the palace. To this end Vespasian drained the lake and in it built the Flavian Amphitheatre, later known as the Colosseum, as a way of distancing himself from the reviled tyrant. Furthermore, Trajan used the brickwork of the palace to build his baths.

But in spite of their worst efforts much remained, and after many years of restoration the Domus Aurea was once again opened to the public. Though 30 rooms are currently open, access to a further 100 is denied. Another 200 rooms remain to be excavated, which gives some idea of the unimaginable vastness of the original project. In September 2009, archaeologists unveiled the possible remains of Nero's rotating banquet hall.

Part 8
ROME
The 'Tourist' sites

Though the Christian pilgrim to Rome is likely to spend most of the time visiting the churches, monuments and museums described so far, nevertheless what may be called the 'tourist' sites will also have a particular appeal in that they, too, contribute to the city's special character and fascination. The aim of this chapter is to focus on the main attractions, though once again time and interest will determine your personal choices.

Fountains, of course, are an important part of Rome's charm and none more so than the **Trevi Fountain** (Piazza di Trevi), the largest and probably the most well-known of them all. Completed in 1762, it is designed around the theme of the ocean, with the dominant figure of Neptune, the sea-god, in the centre. He is flanked by two Tritons representing the two natures of the sea, one whose sea horse is very agitated and the other whose beast is much more placid. The figures in the two side niches symbolise Abundance and Salubrity. The fountain is at the end of the Acqua Vergine, the aqueduct built by Agrippa in 19 BC to bring water into the city from springs some 12 miles away. At the top of the fountain is a relief portraying the legendary young girl who is said to have shown this spring to thirsty Roman soldiers. As to how the fountain received its name, no one is quite sure. Was the young girl's name Trivia? Or, is it to do with the meeting of three roads, *tre vie?* Whatever the explanation, before you leave the fountain do remember to stand with your back to it and throw a coin over your shoulder. You will most surely return – or so it is said!

A short walk from here is another of Rome's 'must see' sights, the **Spanish Steps** (Piazza di Spagna). Like the Trevi fountain they seem to be crowded with people both day and night, especially in the summer, because since the 18th century this has been an area for those who want to be seen as well as to see! The elegant steps take their name from the Spanish Embassy to the Holy See which has been in the Piazza since the 17th century. They were designed in 1720 to link the piazza with the 16th century French church of **Trinita dei Monti** at the top, from where there are some striking views across the city. The steps are seen at their finest in the spring, when they are colourfully decorated with pots of blossoming azaleas. The boat-shaped fountain at the foot of the

The Trevi Fountain

The Spanish Steps

stairway is believed to have been designed by Bernini's less famous father, Pietro, and it, too, is fed by the Acqua Vergine.

On the right, facing the steps, is the **Keats-Shelley Memorial House**, where the poet John Keats died at the age of 25 in 1821 after spending the last few months of his life in Rome. In 1906 the Keats-Shelly Memorial Association was founded and in 1909 the house was turned into a museum and library, with many objects and manuscripts honouring Keats, Shelley, Byron and other British Romantic poets. Both Keats and Shelley are buried in Rome's Protestant Cemetery.

The narrow streets around the Piazza di Spagna are home to some of the city's most exclusive shops. With your back to the steps, walk straight ahead into the **Via Condotti** and you will be able, should you feel so inclined, to contribute to the profits of Armani, Bulgari, Gucci, Louis Vuitton, Yves Saint Laurent and the rest! If not, remember that window-shopping doesn't cost anything.

Alternatively, instead of going straight ahead, turn right up the Via del Babuino and after passing a whole variety of antique shops you will come to the elegant **Piazza del Popolo**. Even in a city of fine squares this one stands out as something special. Set in the old Aurelian Wall is the **Porta del Popolo**, originally known as the Porta Flaminia after the Via Flaminia, constructed in 220 AD to link the Adriatic coast with Rome. So for centuries this gate and square were the main ways into the city for pilgrims and travellers from the north. The inner façade of the gate was re-designed by Bernini in 1655 to commemorate the visit of Queen Christina of Sweden who, after abdicating her throne, came to the city to be received into the Roman Catholic Church from Lutheranism. Adjacent to the gate is the church of **Santa Maria del Popolo**, a building full of art treasures and an absolute 'must' for a visit if you are in this area (see page 38).

At the centre of the piazza is the **Egyptian obelisk**, dating from the 13th century BC and taken from the Sun Temple in Heliopolis in 10 BC by the Emperor Augustus. Up until 1589 it adorned the Circus Maximus, but in that year Pope Sixtus V had it moved to the centre of the square. It was in the early 19th century, when it was re-designed by Giuseppe Valadier, that the piazza took its present oval shape. At the southern end are what appear to be two identical 17th century churches, designed by Carlo Rainaldi, **Santa Maria dei Miracoli** (with the round dome) and **Santa Maria di Montesanto** (with an oval one). The use of different shaped domes was a device employed by Rainaldi, who at all costs wanted to maintain a sense of symmetry at that end of the piazza. So, they are not quite the identical twin churches they appear to be! To the east the square is overlooked by the **Pincio Gardens**, one of the oldest in Rome and adjacent to the Villa Borghese. From here there are splendid panoramas over the city and towards the Vatican.

Running out from the southern end of the square between the two churches is the Via del Corso which links the Piazza del Popolo with the Piazza Venezia. Here is the **Vittorio Emanuele II** monument, built between 1885 and 1911 to honour the first king of a united Italy. This enormous building is something of a joke among Romans, for its brilliant white marble stands out in stark contrast to the city's more muted and subtle colours. 'Kitsch' and 'monstrosity' are two of its descriptions, as are 'wedding cake' and 'typewriter'. Whatever its architectural shortcomings, it certainly stands out as a landmark! There are also fine views from the top. At the front is a huge equestrian statue of Victor Emmanuel himself and behind him is the eternal flame, Italy's memorial to the Unknown Soldier, hence the other name for the monument, *The Altar of the Nation*.

If possible be sure to make time for a visit to the **Piazza Navona**, arguably the most beautiful of all Rome's piazzas and situated in the heart of the city's historic centre. Today, as previously, it is very much a hub of the city's social life. But whereas in the past it would have been flooded each August to provide watery entertainment for all and sundry, now all and sundry come to the piazza to stroll among the artists and musicians, and to enjoy the square's many bars, cafes and restaurants. Day or night, something always seems to be happening!

It takes its oval shape by following the lines of the stadium built by Domitian in 86 AD, which could accommodate 30,000 spectators and was used for various sports and athletic contests *(agones)*, including chariot racing. Variously changed by Domitian's successors, the piazza took on its present shape in the 17th century due to Pope Innocent X commissioning a new palace, church and fountain.

At the centre of the square is the largest of its three fountains, the **Fontana dei Quattro Fiumi** (Fountain of the Four Rivers). Though the commission was first offered to Bernini's great rival, Borromini, it was eventually handed to Bernini. He produced what is probably his finest fountain, designed around four statues representing four great rivers – the Danube, Ganges, Nile and Plate. Notice that the figure depicting the Nile is blindfolded, presumably because at the time its source was unknown. The two other fountains are the **Fontana del Nettuno** (Fountain of Neptune) at the northern end of the square and the **Fontana del Moro** (Fountain of the Moor) at the southern end, whose central figure of the Moor was designed by Bernini.

On the western side, facing Bernini's great statue, is the imposing church of **Sant'Agnese in Agone**. It is thought that originally an 8th century oratory stood on this site which marks the spot where legend says that St. Agnes was martyred at the age of thirteen. Later, in the 12th century, it was consecrated as a church. In 1652 Pope Innocent X, as part of his grand design for the piazza, ordered the church to be enlarged and initially the work was begun by Carlo and Girolamo Rainaldi. However, due to a falling out between them and the

Piazza Navona – Bernini's 'The Four Rivers'

Pope, he handed the commission on to Borromini, who designed the concave façade, the dome and the belfries.

The interior, which is decorated with frescoes, statues and paintings, is in the shape of a Greek cross and has seven altars. The body of Innocent X lies in a crypt to the left of the main altar, and the altar of St. Agnes was designed by Rainaldi. Beneath the church are Roman ruins, reputedly including those of the brothel where St. Agnes is said to have been martyred.

On your various tours around the city it is unlikely that you will miss seeing at some stage the massively rugged **Castel Sant'Angelo**, with its commanding position overlooking the Tiber. Should time permit then a visit is recommended for it represents some 2000 years of Roman history from the Emperor Hadrian onwards and as such is one of the city's most important historical monuments, now serving as the National Museum. Completed in 139 AD as a mausoleum for the Emperor himself, it has over the centuries variously served as a citadel, a prison and a refuge for Popes threatened by turbulent events. Indeed, it is possible to see the corridor built in the 13th century linking it to the Vatican, so providing a ready means of escape for threatened Popes. It took on its role as a museum in the late 19th century.

The Castel takes its name from a vision of the Archangel Michael received by Pope Gregory the Great during a time of plague in the 6th century and as he was leading a procession across the nearby bridge. The angel was seen sheathing a sword and this was taken to indicate the end of the plague. Entrance is via Hadrian's original ramp and once inside there is much to see, including prison cells, storerooms, a library, various collections of ceramics, paintings and weapons, a treasury and sumptuously decorated papal apartments. Be sure not to miss the *Sala di Apollo* and the *Sala Paolina*, both with the most beautiful frescoes. From the ramparts there are stupendous outlooks over the city and this is where Tosca, in Puccini's opera, threw herself to her death.

Leading across the Tiber to the Castel is the **Ponte Sant'Angelo**, probably the most striking bridge in the city. Although most of it was constructed during the 17th and 19th centuries, nevertheless the three central arches date back to the time of Hadrian, who had the bridge built to link his mausoleum with the city centre. The ten white angels with their flowing robes, which embellish the balustrades, were all designed by Bernini, and each one holds an instrument relating to Christ's Passion.

Clearly, everything so far described in these chapters will be viewed by the pilgrim and visitor during daylight. Yet in addition, a tour of the city at night has much to commend it, for to see all these churches and monuments beautifully floodlit has its own special atmosphere and is a most memorable experience.

Outside of Rome there are a variety of places which could repay a visit and the option of doing that will depend once again on the content of your itinerary

Rome

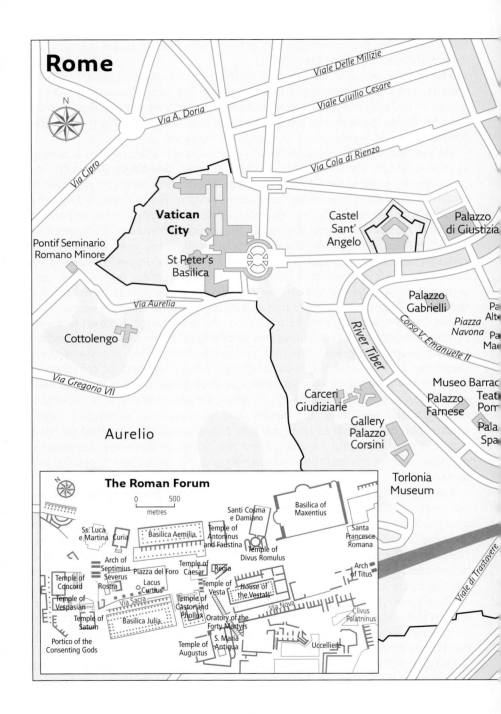

Viale Delle Milizie

Viale Giulio Cesare

Via A. Doria

Via Cipro

Via Cola di Rienzo

N

Vatican City

St Peter's Basilica

Pontif Seminario Romano Minore

Via Aurelia

Cottolengo

Via Gregorio VII

Aurelio

Castel Sant' Angelo

Palazzo di Giustizia

Palazzo Gabrielli

Piazza Navona

Corso V. Emanuele II

River Tiber

Pa Alt

Pa Mac

Carceri Giudiziarie

Gallery Palazzo Corsini

Museo Barrac

Palazzo Farnese

Teat Pom

Pala Spa

Torlonia Museum

Viale di Trastavere

The Roman Forum

N

0   500
metres

Ss. Luca e Martina

Curia

Basilica Aemilia

Santi Cosma e Damiano

Temple of Antoninus and Faustina

Basilica of Maxentius

Santa Francesca Romana

Temple of Divus Romulus

Arch of Septimius Severus

Rostra

Piazza del Foro

Temple of Caesar

Regia

Arch of Titus

Temple of Concord

Lacus Curtius

Temple of Vesta

House of the Vestals

Via Nova

Temple of Vespasian

Via Sacra

Temple of Castor and Phollux

Clivus Palatninus

Temple of Saturn

Basilica Julia

Oratory of the Forty Martyrs

Uccelliere

Portico of the Consenting Gods

Temple of Augustus

S. Maria Antiqua

Santa Maria del Popolo

Villa Borghese

Galoppatoio

Piazza Fiume

Via Nomentana

Viale C. Pretorio

National Central Library

Mausoleo di Augusto

Trinità dei Monti

Fountain of the Bees

Via XX Settembre

Triton Fountain

National Museum of Rome

Via del Corso

Quirinale

Via Quirinale

Via Marsala

Rome Terminal Station

Trevi Fountain

Via Nazionale

Via Giovanni Giolitti

theon

Palazzo Colonna

Santa Maria Maggiore

alazzo Doria Pamphili

Palazzo Venezia

Piazza Vittorio Emanuele II

Palazzo Mattei

Capitoline Museums

Via G. Lanza

eatre of rcellus

Via Cavour

San Pietro in Vincoli

M. Esquilino

Via Merulana

Palazzo dei Conservatori

er nd

Palatine Museum

Arch of Constantine

Colosseum

Via Labicana

Santa Maria in Cosmedin

M. Palatino

Via di S. Gregorio

Via Claudia

ver Tiber

Via Amba Aradam

San Giovanni in Laterano

Viale Aventino

Via delle Terme di Caracalla

Circus Maximus

0   500
metres

and your own predilections. But if there is an opportunity to escape from the city as the Romans themselves do, then here are three possibilities.

The first is the Pope's own summer retreat, **Castel Gandolfo**, a short distance to the south-east, set in the Alban hills and overlooking Lake Albano. Both the 17th century **Papal Palace**, with its magnificent gardens (though closed to the public) and Vatican observatory, as well as the adjoining Villa Barberini are part of the independent Vatican City State. Facing the Papal residence is the main square, **Piazza del Plebiscito**, a compact and cosy area with bars, cafes and small shops. In its centre is yet another elegant Bernini fountain, and in one corner is the lovely church of San Tommaso di Villanova, also by Bernini. A walk round the side of the church brings you to a terrace with views across the lake.

Another excursion could be to **Frascati**, which, like Castel Gandolfo, is one of the towns in a region south of Rome which since the Middle Ages has been known as the 'Castelli Romani'. Because of its location, Frascati is a town with a healthy climate and has become most popularly known for its light, white wine. According to those in the know, the wine that you drink here is somewhat superior to the variety on sale in your local supermarket! Though the town suffered severe damage in World War II, its buildings have now been mostly restored.

Apart from its wine, the chief delight of Frascati, however, lies in its many villas dating back to the 16th and 17th centuries. These stately buildings, set in magnificent gardens, belonged to old noble families. One of the most impressive of these is the **Villa Aldobrandini** which, with its dominant position, can provide stunning views of Rome from its terrace. Though it is not possible to visit the villa itself, the gardens are open to the public and well worth discovering for their complex of cascades, fountains, niches and statues, a true 'Water Theatre'.

One further relatively convenient option is **Tivoli** (ancient Tibur), picturesquely situated to the east of Rome on the western slopes the Sabine hills. Conquered by the Romans in 338 BC it soon became a favourite getaway of Rome's moneyed classes, who built their summer retreats here due to its fresher climate. Even now it is still one of the most popular daytrips from the city.

Today's visitors will find much to maintain their interest. The 4th century BC walls are still visible, as are remains of temples dating from about 2nd century BC, some of which were once incorporated into churches. The two most significant temples to be seen today are the rectangular **Temple of Sybil**, which was transformed in the Middle Ages into the no-longer visible Church of St. George, and the round-based **Temple of Vestra**, which dominates the valley now occupied by the Villa Gregoriana. This particular temple was originally formed of 18 fluted columns, though today only 10 can be seen. At the top of the town is the **Rocca Pia**, a 15th century castle built by Pope Pius II. Also to be seen is the church of **San Silvestro**, a Romanesque building of the 12th century with some pleasing frescoes from the second half of that century. In addition there is the **Cathedral of San Lorenzo**, completely rebuilt in 1635 to replace the earlier 12th century building, from which the Romanesque bell-tower still remains. Inside there is a 13th century wood-carving of the *Descent from the Cross*, a fine example of medieval carving, as well as a priceless 12th century *Triptych of the Saviour*, painted on wood.

The most famous site in Tivoli is undoubtedly the 16th century **Villa d'Este**. Extravagant though it may be, it is certainly a Renaissance gem. Constructed in the 1550s for Cardinal Ippolito d'Este, the son of Lucretia Borgia, it was built over a Benedictine convent, its courtyard being the cloister of the convent. Although the villa contains rooms lavishly decorated with frescoes, yet again the main attraction is the beautiful gardens, composed almost entirely of water features. There are fountains of every description, including a miniature watery reproduction of Rome. Among these famous fountains are the *One Hundred Fountains, the Fountain of the Dragon* and *the Fountain of the Hydraulic Organ*, though it no longer plays music as it once did.

Down in the valley is the **Villa Gregoriana**, also worth as visit. Once again it is the garden and the waterfalls which are the most striking attractions, with the River Aniene cascading down into the *Grande Cascata*. It is also near here that you will find the temples of Vesta and Sybil.

A short distance out of Tivoli is the largest and finest of all Roman villas, the **Villa Adriana**. Mind you, to do it justice would take several hours as it is a massive complex of buildings and gardens. It was the brain-child of the Emperor Hadrian, who determined in 118 AD to create a country retreat for himself in the valley beneath the hill on which Tivoli is situated. Completed in 134 AD, it is composed of monumental buildings, roads, pools, baths, libraries, theatres and temples. Being the widely-travelled Emperor that he was, Hadrian was keen to reproduce here some of the wonders he had seen in Egypt and Greece, and rather than grouping them all together he spread them throughout the site. Fortunately there is a model on display which helps you to appreciate the full extent of this very remarkable complex.

Part 9
ASSISI

Situated to the north of Rome in the central part of Italy is the delightful region of Umbria. It may be gentler in form than neighbouring Tuscany, but is most certainly no less enchanting, with its fertile valleys and beautiful medieval hill-top villages, many of which could be the setting for an opera. Old towns like Perugia, Spoleto and Orvieto along with hill-towns like Gubbio, Montefalco and Spello all add to the very special character of an area which dates back to the 8th century BC, when it became the homeland of the Umbrians. Later it developed as a settlement for Etruscans and ultimately came under Roman control. It was here too, at Lake Trasimeno, that Hannibal defeated the Roman consul Gaius Flaminius in 217 BC.

Most groups visiting Rome will want to visit the beautiful, medieval town of Assisi. Though its origins go back to Roman times, what the town is today undoubtedly dates back to its development during the Middle Ages. Set on the side of Monte Subasio, this is where St. Francis was born in 1182. Whether as a

Assisi towers above the Plains of Umbria

day visit from Rome, or even, for example, en route to or from Florence, the birth-place of the saint is surely an essential on every Christian pilgrim's list of places to be visited.

THE BACKGROUND

Though his story is well-known to many, a brief rehearsal of the main features of his life will set the scene for what you are about to see and experience. The son of a wealthy merchant, he was baptised Giovanni but subsequently renamed Francesco by his father, probably as an expression of the latter's love for France. Because of his father's wealth Francis spent much of his early life enjoying a very rich, easy-going existence in which there seemed to be no limit to the pursuit of pleasure, though at the same time he appears to have been regarded among his peers as a happy and charming person, who also had the qualities of a born leader.

At that time Italy was divided into several small states which regularly waged war on each other. In 1201 Assisi went to war with its long-time and nearby enemy of Perugia, during which confrontation Francis was taken hostage and held in captivity for a year. The experience of imprisonment and a period of ill-health associated with it seem to have begun a process of change in him. However, some 4 years later in 1205, we find Francis still looking for military glory as he prepared to take part in a campaign against Apulia. But as the result of a dream he abandoned his intention of becoming a knight and returned to Assisi.

While praying in the dilapidated church of San Damiano near Assisi in 1206, he believed he heard Christ speaking to him from the crucifix and instructing him to repair his church. This he took very literally and by his own endeavours began the task of rebuilding San Damiano. To raise money he took some of his father's cloth and sold it. So incensed was his father that he dragged Francis before the bishop, who, in his wisdom, told him to return the money because God would provide.

At this point Francis made the life-changing decision to renounce his rights and possessions, including his clothing, so that he could help the sick and needy and those whom society considered to be outcasts. At the same time he appears to have realised that the vision instructing him to rebuild God's church had wider implications than just the fabric of San Damiano. So he began travelling and preaching, and slowly companions gathered round him wanting to follow his way. His aim for both himself and his followers was to live by the Gospel, emphasising simplicity, poverty and humility as they declared the love of God in Christ by word and action. Pope Innocent III gave his approval to the brotherhood, which Francis referred to as the Friars Minor, and they made their base at the chapel of the Porziuncola at Santa Maria degli Angeli. So began the Franciscan movement.

In 1212, Francis was joined by a young woman from Assisi named Clare, also from a wealthy background. She had heard him preaching, determined to live the Christian life in a more radical way and so became one of his loyal followers. On Palm Sunday 1212 she secretly left her home and met Francis at the Porziuncola. There he cut off her hair and she exchanged her fine clothes for the simple tunic of a disciple of Francis. As others joined her, including her sister, Agnes, (her mother and another sister joined her some years later), Clare founded a sisterhood, which became known as the Poor Ladies or Poor Clares, an Order committed to living out the Christian way through a life of total poverty and humility. Appropriately enough it was at San Damiano where Francis established them and it was here that she later died in 1253.

Two years later she was canonised by Pope Alexander IV. Throughout her life not only was Clare the inspiration of her Order in its mission, but was also an invaluable source of support and encouragement for Francis himself.

As the Franciscan Order grew in subsequent years, Francis had to delegate responsibility to others, eventually handing over the leadership of the Order. Much of the rest of his life was spent travelling and preaching in and beyond Italy. He even wanted to preach in Syria and Morocco, but was prevented by shipwreck in the one instance and illness in the other, though he did spend some time in Spain. In 1219 he travelled to the Holy Land with the 5th Crusade, where he tried to convert the Sultan of Egypt.

His final years were dogged by ill-health, during which time he was nursed by the ever-loyal Clare, and in 1224 he received the stigmata (the wounds of Christ). Francis died in the Porziuncola in the evening of the 3rd October 1226 and was canonised in 1228, later becoming the patron saint of Italy.

THE TOWN

Despite the earthquake of September 1997, Assisi remains extremely well-preserved and rich in history. With its Roman roots, its delightful medieval streets and houses, its treasures of art and architecture, it is indeed one of Italy's finest pilgrim and tourist sites, and as such was added to Unesco's World Heritage List in 2000. It would be difficult for anyone, whether pilgrim or tourist, to resist the very special appeal of the town's distinctive atmosphere.

Because the town centre is enclosed within the walls, much the easiest access to it is from the eastern end, through the Porta Nuova. Entry though this gate is greatly assisted by escalators from the coach parking areas. Then, as you walk into the town, you can observe the medieval character in much of its architecture. The various façades with pointed arches all date from the 12th and 14th centuries.

One of the first churches you will come to is the **Basilica di Santa Chiara**, the burial place of St. Clare. Though, like the Duomo and San Francesco, it

The Medieval Setting of Assisi

suffered damage in the earthquake, Santa Chiara is now restored. It was built between 1257 and 1265 on the site of the earlier church of San Giorgio. This was the church where the body of St. Francis was buried until its removal in 1230 to the Basilica named after him, and where in 1228 he was canonised by Pope Gregory IX. Santa Chiara's Italian gothic-style has an appropriate simplicity about it, very much in keeping with the life-styles of both Clare and Francis himself. Before entering the Basilica, notice the way in which the exterior is adorned with alternate strips of white and pink stone, with massive supporting arches on either side.

Once inside, and as you face the high altar, the chapel on the left is dedicated to *St. Agnes*, the sister of Clare, both of whom are represented among the various saints portrayed in the early 14th century frescoes on the vault. In the left transept is a Nativity scene, believed to be the work of one of Giotto's students, and in the right transept there is a panel painted with the 'Life of St. Clare' by the so-called 'Maestro di Santa Chiara' (13th century). There are also frescoes depicting St. Clare and various New Testament scenes. Staying with the right hand aisle leads to two Chapels which are all that remain from the original church of San Giorgio, the *Chapel of the Crucifix* and the *Chapel of the Sacrament*. The former is so named because of its 12th century wooden crucifix, which tradition declares to be the one originally hanging in the church of San Damiano and from which St. Francis heard the invitation to rebuild the church. There are also some holy relics including tunics worn by Francis and Clare, as well as a shirt which she embroidered and some of her hair. In the adjoining Chapel of the Sacrament the walls are covered with frescoes representing various scenes from the life of Christ.

Returning to the nave from the Chapel of the Crucifix brings you to a flight of stairs taking you down to *the crypt*. Here in a raised sarcophagus lie the remains of St. Clare. After her death in 1253 she was buried in the then Church of San Giorgio. Later, in 1260, her body was buried deep beneath the high altar of the new church built in her honour, Santa Chiara. It was only in 1850, having remained hidden and inaccessible for six centuries, that Clare's tomb was found after an extensive search and in 1872 transferred to its present position.

On leaving the Basilica, and before progressing further into the town, do take time to enjoy the views from the piazza. Looking one way will give you a sweeping panorama of the broad Umbrian valley below Assisi and then, turning your back to this, will enable you to look up towards the top of the town, with its narrow tiered streets, alleyways and terracotta roofs, to the great dominating fortress of Rocca Maggiore.

Moving on from here along the Corso Mazzini brings you to the **Piazza del Comune**, the main square of Assisi, which is the heart of its cultural, political and social life. Presumably, too, this was where Francis spent a good deal of his time in his care-free younger days. Beneath the piazza is a passageway to the remains of what may have been the town's **Roman Forum**, though there is some debate about this, where among other things you can see the base of the steps leading up to the original temple above.

As you enter the piazza one of the first buildings to catch the eye is the outstanding exterior of the **Church of Santa Maria sopra Minerva**. Originally a 1st century BC Roman Temple dedicated to Minerva, though Castor and Phollux have also been suggested as possibilities, the striking façade, with its six fluted columns supporting Corinthian capitals, has survived the centuries exceptionally well, making it the most important remaining Roman structure in Assisi. The flight of steps leading up to the entrance would have been longer in Roman times given that the original paving was somewhat lower than the current level. In 1539 the inner sanctum of the temple was transformed into a Christian church, and during the 17th century further Baroque-style additions were made.

To the left of Santa Maria is the **Torre del Popolo**, Tower of the People, a symbol of Assisi's freedom and autonomy. It was begun during the second-half of the 13th century, continued in stages and finally completed in 1305. The clock was not built until the mid-15th century. In 1926 the Bell of Lauds was added, a gift to Assisi from the towns of Italy. Adjacent to this is the 13th century **Palazzo del Capitano del Popolo**, the headquarters of the commander of the city militia, who was responsible for maintaining public order.

On the opposite side of the Piazza is the **Palazzo dei Priori**, part of a complex of buildings which housed the local government offices and which is still the Town Hall today. Dating back to the 13th century this was the first public building to be erected in the Piazza del Commune. Also on this southern side is the **Pinacoteca**, the municipal art gallery which contains frescoes from various schools.

If you stand in the Piazza with this southern side on your right and facing back towards Santa Chiara, then take a small street at the top right-hand corner of the square. This will bring you down to the **Chiesa Nuova**, a small church built in 1615 with the financial help of Philip III, King of Spain. In the shape of a Greek cross it is constructed on the remains of what is believed to be the home of Francis's family and where he himself would have grown up in his youth. Externally there is one large dome and four smaller ones around it. Once inside there is a small room on the left, said to be the place where Francis was imprisoned by his father for taking, without permission, cloth to sell in order to repair the church of San Damiano. Visitors can go through the convent to see some of the rooms in which Francis spent his childhood.

In the piazza outside the church is a statue of Francis' parents, with his mother holding the chains with which his father tried to bind Francis to the wealthy way of life he had planned for his son. Going down the left hand side of Chiesa Nuova leads to the Oratory of **San Francesco Piccolino**, where according to tradition his mother, Monna Pica, gave birth to him.

A short walk down from the Piazza della Chiesa Nuova is the Piazza del Vescovado and the church of **Santa Maria Maggiore**. Founded in the 10th century it is possible, because of the Roman remains beneath it, that this may have been the site of the original Cathedral of Assisi dating back to the 4th century. Be that as it may, Cathedral status was passed from here to San Rufino in 1036. The present building is 12th century. The exterior has a strikingly simple Romanesque façade with a small rose window, and the Bell Tower is 14th century. As for the interior, the nave, semi-circular apse and sacristy still have remains of frescoes from the 14th and 15th centuries. It is possible that at one time the walls were completely covered in frescoes. The crypt dates back to the previous church and is the only part of the earlier structure remaining. Nearby would have been the Palace of the Bishop and this remained so even after Santa Maria was no longer the Cathedral. Notably it was here that Francis, in the presence of Bishop Guido and others, publicly renounced his inheritance and committed himself to a life of simplicity and poverty.

From the Piazza del Comune instead of turning right down the southern side to Chiesa Nuova, take the Via S Rufino up the hill from the top left-hand corner. Though it is something of a climb this will bring you to the **Duomo**, the church of **San Rufino**. There are those who believe that this might have been the site of the town's Roman Forum. However, what is not in doubt is its Cathedral status from the 11th century onwards and that Francis and Clare were both baptised here.

The church was initially erected to house the body of St. Rufino, the first Bishop of Assisi who was martyred in 238 AD when he was drowned in the nearby Chiascio river. There was probably a church on this site in the 8th century and there are those who would argue for an even earlier date of the 5th century. The present building was begun in 1140, though there was a prior one in the 11th century, and took more than 100 years to complete, not being consecrated until 1253. The superb Romanesque façade is adorned with three rose windows, a large central one surrounded by symbols of the Four Evangelists, and two smaller ones on either side. Both the square bell-tower and the crypt are the only surviving parts of the previous 11th century building. The interior was drastically modified in 1571 which gave it a late Renaissance rather than Romanesque style, but still to be seen at the beginning of the right hand aisle is the *Baptismal Font* where Francis and Clare were baptised. Also on the right is the *Chapel of the Sacrament*, containing several 17th century paintings representing the Old and New Testaments. The body of St. Rufino is buried under the high altar, and the apse contains a fine wooden choir. In the *Crypt* there are remnants of 11th and 12th century frescoes and a Roman sarcophagus which held the body of St. Rufino.

While in this part of the town it is possible, time and energy permitting of course, to go even further up and visit the **Rocca Maggiore**. If you continue beyond the Piazza San Rufino, to left there is a flight of steps which will bring you eventually to the Via della Rocca and to the fortress. High above the town it both dominates the area around and provides spectacular views over the Spoleto valley.

Given its strategic position, it is likely that a fortress was first built here in ancient times, during the era of the Umbrian tribes. Another fortress was subsequently built in 1174 and it was here that the future Emperor Frederick II spent several years of his childhood and in 1197, at the age of 3, was baptised in the Duomo. After being destroyed by the Assisians it remained a ruin until it was rebuilt during the second part of the 14th century when Cardinal Albornoz, on the Pope's orders, overhauled the defensive system of the Papal States. During the 15th century the 12-sided tower was added and the keep restored, and between 1535–1538 Pope Paul III built the round tower near the main gate. It is possible to visit the keep, the soldiers' quarters and rooms belonging to the residential part.

Returning to the Piazza del Comune and taking the Via San Francesco leads to the great monument of the **Basilica di San Francesco**, with its gorgeous works of art, the second most important Basilica in Italy after St. Peter's, Rome, and indeed, one of the most important churches in the world. On the way there, and wherever you walk in Assisi, do not forget to take notice of the buildings and side streets which epitomise the charm of the town. The Basilica consists of two churches, the earlier Lower Church and the later Upper Church. In the earthquake of 1997 which devastated parts of central Italy, the Lower Church remained unscathed but the Upper one experienced extensive damage, in the process of which four people were killed as the ceiling collapsed. Some 2,300 sq. feet of paintings were damaged, including those by Cimabue and his assistants, and the famous *Life of St. Francis* frescoes. But a remarkable programme of restoration was quickly set in motion both to renovate the frescoes and to repair and strengthen the structure, so making it more earthquake resistant.

THE BASILICA OF ST FRANCIS

Two years after the death of Francis and the day after his canonisation, Pope Gregory IX laid the foundation stone of the Lower Church on 17 July 1228, and two years later, in 1230, the body of Francis was brought here from the then church of San Giorgio to be laid at rest in the new church – a remarkable feat of construction in record time. The Upper Church was begun shortly afterwards and both churches were consecrated by Pope Innocent IV in 1253, though it took another 100 years or so to decorate the church with its famous frescoes, in due course making it one of the finest repositories of Italian painting. It was not until 1754 that the church was granted Basilica status.

The Basilica of St Francis

Much of the credit for the building of the Lower Church must undoubtedly go to Brother Elia, who even during Francis's lifetime played a prominent role in the early development of the Franciscan movement. Certainly, in the latter part of the saint's life, he undertook much of the responsibility for organising the Order. After Francis's death and even before his canonisation, Brother Elia appears to have had plans for an appropriate church to house the tomb of the saint and it was his vision and energy which saw the lower church completed in only two years. But then came the building of the Upper Church, seeming to make the statement that here was a saint who needed not one but two churches as a celebration of his renown. Over the next century the Basilica was decorated by some of Italy's finest painters, among them Cimabue, Giotto, Simone Martini and Pietro Lorenzetti, though some may think its sumptuous character to be in stark contrast to the simple life-style of Francis himself. Be that as it may, this is how those of that time wished to recognise the saint's greatness. It should, however, also be pointed out that the function of such painting was not merely aesthetic, to make a church look more decorative, but also to be part of its liturgical and religious function as an expression of its preaching.

Although the lower part is low-ceilinged, crypt-like and dark while the upper part is lofty, spacious and light, the buildings give the impression of being an integrated whole. This is largely due to the way in which the upper part of the Basilica faithfully follows the lines of the lower. Both are built to a 'T' shape, representing the simple 'Tau' cross favoured by Francis and his followers. Nevertheless, further additions and modifications were made during succeeding centuries.

As you approach the Basilica from Via San Francesco, the first thing which will strike you as you look across the lawn is the façade of the Upper Church, an early example of Italian Gothic, with its large rose window surrounded by symbols of the four evangelists. Nowadays it is hard to imagine the Lower Church as a building on its own, yet however tempting it may be to begin your visit at the upper level, there is much to recommend that you should go down and begin at the lower one, if for no other reason than to see yourself as following in the steps of those first pilgrims who had toiled their way here to pay homage to Francis and catch sight of his tomb beneath the altar.

THE LOWER CHURCH

The way into the Romanesque Lower Church is through a 13th century Gothic portal under a Renaissance porch. This leads you into the large entrance transept, a later addition to the original building. As you walk into it you will see on the left the *Chapel of St. Sebastian* and on the right some Gothic tombs as well as the *Chapel of St. Anthony*. Facing you on the far apse wall is the *Chapel of St. Catherine*, with frescoes depicting the life of St. Catherine.

From here turn your attention to the nave which was the first part of the church to be frescoed. The various side chapels were not part of the original church and were built largely to accommodate the influx of pilgrims, but unfortunately their construction destroyed the sequence of frescoes which previously adorned the side walls. Facing towards the altar, the frescoes on the *left side* represent the life of St. Francis, namely, St. Francis stripping himself and so renouncing his paternal and worldly wealth; the dream of Pope Innocent III in which he pictures Francis supporting the church; the saint preaching to the birds; his stigmata; his funeral. On the *right side* is a parallel cycle representing the Passion of Christ – Christ is stripped of his clothes; the crucifixion with weeping figures; his body is taken down from the Cross; the burial; the appearance on the road to Emmaus. These cycles, which are dated about 1260, were clearly designed to stress the link between Francis and Christ, and their unknown creator is identified only as the 'Maestro di Francesco'.

Two of the side chapels in particular are worth attention. One is the Gothic-style *Chapel of St. Martin*, the first chapel on the left as you begin to walk down the nave. This is possibly the most beautiful of all the chapels, especially because of the wonderful cycle of 10 frescoes painted by the Sienese master-painter, Simone Martini, between 1312–15. These depict the life of St. Martin of Tours in the 4th century, who like Francis himself, came from a well-to-do family (his father was an officer in the Roman army), had dreams of military glory, and on meeting a poor beggar cut his own cloak in half to share it with him. It is said that the next night he had a dream of Christ himself wearing the part of the cloak he had given away. The incident of the beggar and the subsequent dream are portrayed in the first two panels on the bottom left-hand side. The rest of the cycle progresses upwards.

The other chapel for a possible visit is the last one on the right, the *Chapel of St. Mary Magdalene*. This was decorated about 1309 due to the generosity of Teobaldo Pantini, the Bishop of Assisi. The paintings are based on stories about Mary taken from the Gospels as well as popular legends about her. Scenes to look out for are, on the left wall, the *'Dinner with the Pharisee'* and the *'Raising of Lazarus'* – notice bystanders covering their noses at the smell! – and on the right wall, the *'Noli me Tangere' ('Do not touch me'),* the meeting of Mary with the Risen Christ in the garden. There was a time when it was generally accepted that the paintings were undoubtedly by Giotto and his school, but more recently there has been much debate among art historians as to the authenticity not only of these frescoes but also of others attributed to him, particularly the St. Francis cycle in the Upper Church. On the whole it is probably fair to say that it is the frescoes in the Lower Church which most reflect his style, whether done by him personally or by members of his school, possibly even as a collaborative effort of both.

Halfway along the nave are steps leading down to the *Tomb of St. Francis*. The crypt in which the tomb is placed was excavated in 1818, mainly to verify that it was still below the high altar. Originally the tomb was open for veneration, but during the 15th century it was sealed off for fear of the saint's relics being stolen. His remains are still encapsulated in the original stone sarcophagus, which is itself enclosed by iron grating. The tomb is flanked by niches containing the remains of four of Francis's most devoted companions. There is also a perpetually burning votive lamp, the oil for which is provided annually by different regions of Italy.

Returning back up to the Lower Church there is now the opportunity to discover the area of the High Altar and the two transepts. Standing at the High Altar with your back to the apse and facing down the nave, look above you to the ceiling vault and in front of you, nearest the nave, is the *Allegory of Poverty*, showing Francis marrying the Madonna Poverty, who is portrayed by a woman in rags. On the right is the *Allegory of Obedience*, with a yoke being placed on the shoulders of a friar flanked by humility and prudence, and at the top is a yoked Francis between two angels. On the left is the *Allegory of Chastity*, with Chastity represented by a woman locked in a tower from which flies a white flag, the symbol of purity. Outside the castle Francis is seen with a Friar, a Poor

Clare, and a Tertiary, the three Franciscan Orders. The fourth panel is behind you, nearest to the apse, and its theme is the *Glory of St. Francis*, with Francis sitting on a throne and surrounded by angels. Again we are faced with a kind of art historian's 'whodunit' – Giotto or not Giotto, or maybe even a dedicated disciple of the master? Whatever the queries about authorship, there can be no doubt that they are masterpieces of 14th century painting.

With your back to the nave and facing the Altar, turn to the *right transept*. This is beautifully decorated with scenes from the childhood of Christ, possibly by Giotto himself or a member of his school. On the *right side* of the vaulting are easily identifiable episodes, looking from top to bottom – *The Annunciation, The Visitation, The Nativity, The Adoration of the Magi, The Presentation of Jesus in the Temple*. There is also a *Crucifixion* here with St. Francis at the foot of the Cross. On the *left wall* of the vaulting, again from top to bottom, are *The Flight into Egypt, The Massacre of the Innocents, Jesus debating in the Temple, The Holy Family's return to Nazareth*. Among other paintings in this transept are, on the bottom right, a large painting by the Florentine master, Cimabue, portraying the *Madonna in Majesty*, seated on a throne and surrounded by angels, as well as a portrait of *St. Francis* closely resembling his description by Thomas of Celano, and the figures of five Saints done by Simone Martini. At the end of this transept is the *Chapel of St. Nicholas*, built in the latter part of the 13th century and containing frescoes portraying events from the life of St. Nicholas.

From a doorway in this transept it is possible to gain access to the *Chapter House*, where relics of St. Francis are on display. These include a patten and chalice used by him, various items of clothing – a hair-shirt, tunic and slippers, the stone on which his head rested in his tomb, an ivory horn given to him as a gift from the Sultan of Egypt, the confirmation of the Rule of St. Francis sent to him by Pope Honorius II in 1223, and a piece of parchment signed by Francis.

Returning into the main body of the Lower Church it is now time to discover the *left transept*. In crossing the church to it, as you pass through the apse notice the beautiful inlaid wooden choir (1471) and the fresco of the *Last Judgement* by Cesare Sermei (1623). The marvellous paintings of the Passion of Christ in the left transept were done by Pietro Lorenzetti in the 1320s. Standing with your back to the High Altar and facing the Chapel of St. John the Baptist, on the *right-hand vault* the scenes from top to bottom are *The Entry into Jerusalem, The Last Supper, Jesus washing the Disciples' Feet, The Garden of Gethsemane, Judas hangs himself, St. Francis receives the Stigmata*. On the *left-hand side wall* at the top are *The Scourging of Jesus* and *The Carrying of the Cross*, and beneath these a large, but damaged *Crucifixion*. On the walls around the archway as you look into the Chapel of St. John are, bottom left and right, *Christ taken down from the Cross* (note the Tau Cross) and *The Burial in the Tomb*, and top left and right, *The Descent into Limbo* and *The Resurrection*. Before leaving here to go to the Upper Church make sure that beneath the large Crucifixion you see the picture known as the *Sunset Madonna*, so-called because it receives the best light at sunset. The figures on either side are St. John and St. Francis, the latter showing the stigmata.

THE UPPER CHURCH

To access the Upper Church, either retrace your steps out of the Lower Church by the way you came in and then walk up to it, entering through the main upper doorway, or use the internal stairs on either side of the apse behind the High Altar. Using these stairs will first bring you out of the church to a terrace which overlooks the 15th century cloister and from here more stairs will lead you to the Upper Church, though en route you may want to divert to the gift shop! Finally, you will come out into the upper part of the Basilica by the altar.

Immediately the visitor is struck by the Gothic loftiness and lightness of the Upper Church, such a marked contrast with what has just been experienced. Built in the shape of a Latin cross it carefully follows the plan of the Lower Church. Because it has only a nave and no side aisles, this helps to emphasise the importance of the paintings on the side walls. Tempting though it may be to begin at once with the nave frescoes, it may preferable to start by exploring the apse and transepts where you are. Part of the splendid illumination of the church is due to the 13th century stained glass windows set in the apse, and these can be seen if you stand facing the altar with your back to the nave. Still looking in that direction, note, too, the papal throne at the rear of the apse and the magnificent early 15th century inlaid choir detailing scenes of still life, books and musical instruments. The apse itself is decorated with frescoes attributed to Cimabue, illustrating scenes from the life of the Virgin Mary. The *left* part of the transept contains five *Apocalyptic Scenes*, *St. Michael and the Dragon*, and a wonderful *Crucifixion* in which once again St. Francis is shown kneeling at the foot of the Cross. Unfortunately, oxidisation in the pigments has badly damaged some of these frescoes. In the *right* part are episodes from the life of St. Peter. These transept frescoes are generally ascribed to Cimabue and his assistants. Above you, on the cross vaulting between the left and right parts of the transept, are paintings of the *Four Evangelists.*

Turning now to the nave itself and standing with your back to the altar, you will notice that the side walls are covered in paintings. The upper part of the left wall contains scenes from the Old Testament, and that on the right scenes from the New, some of which have been damaged and others destroyed. Though they are less conspicuous than the much lower and more famous St. Francis cycle, they are still worthy of attention in spite of the severe damage to a number of them. So, starting from the altar end but with your back to the altar and facing down the nave towards the main entrance, the uppermost frescoes on the *left wall* are painted around the theme of creation, *The Creation of the World, The Creation of Adam, The Creation of Eve, The original Sin, The banishment from Paradise* and fragments of *The killing of Abel,* with two intermediate frescoes having been destroyed. Immediately below these is another Old Testament sequence dealing with the creation of a new order, beginning with *The Building of the Ark, The Entry of Noah and the animals into the Ark* (much damaged, but you can see part of a gangway from the land to the boat), *Abraham preparing to slay Isaac* (again much damaged, but still possible to make out what it represents), *The Angels visiting Abraham, Isaac blesses Jacob* (both of these are damaged), *Esau in front of Isaac, Joseph let down into the Well by his brothers* (much of the centre is damaged) and *Joseph makes himself known to his brothers.*

On the opposite side of the nave, on the *right wall*, a number of the New Testament scenes have suffered a similar fate to those on the left in that they are partially or almost completely destroyed. However, that does not detract from an appreciation of those which can be viewed more or less in their entirety. If the theme of the upper cycle on the left wall represented Creation and the Old Adam, those on this wall are to do with the New Adam and the New Creation. Beginning once again from the altar end with your back to the altar, the uppermost paintings are *The Annunciation, The Visit to Elizabeth* (much destroyed apart from a few fragments), *The Nativity, The Adoration of the Magi* (a little damaged), *The Presentation in the Temple, The Flight into Egypt* (almost completely missing), *The Debating in the Temple* (badly damaged) and a damaged *Baptism of Jesus.* The second cycle, just below these, represents the Passion of Jesus – *The Wedding at Cana, The Raising of Lazarus* (so badly damaged that it is impossible to recognise its theme), *The Betrayal of Judas, Christ before Pilate* (almost impossible to discern), *Jesus being led to Calvary, The Crucifixion, The Burial of Jesus, The Women at the Tomb* (much damaged), *The Ascension* (obvious in spite of its damage), *The Descent of the Holy Spirit.* It is thought that most of these paintings were done by the followers of Cimabue and also members of the Roman school. There is a possibility that the frescoes relating to Isaac may have been by Giotto himself (1290–1295).

Beneath all these paintings is the main appeal of the Upper Church – the famous cycle of 28 frescoes portraying the **Life of St. Francis**, without doubt one of the finest of such cycles. Between 1260–1263 St. Bonaventure, who joined the Franciscan Order as a young man, wrote his 'Life of St. Francis' and the paintings closely follow the story of the saint as set out in that work. As with the upper paintings, with your back to the altar, the sequence begins near the altar on the *left wall* and then proceeds clockwise around the nave. Each scene is complete in itself, a particular episode in the story, and Francis can be identified first by his halo and then also, except in the earliest frescoes, by his brown habit.

The Church of St Clare

1. *Homage of a Simple Man*
This episode is clearly set in the Piazza del Comune, with the Temple of Minerva in the background, and shows an ordinary citizen of Assisi spreading his cloak in front of Francis, as a sign that he is worthy to receive honour for what he is yet to accomplish. Francis is identifiable by his halo but in this picture is still wearing the clothes of a wealthy merchant's son.

2. *St. Francis gives his cloak to a Poor Man.*
Francis meets a destitute and poorly clothed nobleman, and out of compassion offers his own cloak to him. This dates back to the time after Francis' imprisonment in Perugia and his subsequent illness. The representation of a city in the upper left-hand corner suggests that the incident took place near Assisi.

3. *The Dream of a Palace*
During the early years of his life Francis longed to achieve great things as a knight. In a dream he sees a splendid palace filled with knightly armour bearing the sign of the Cross. Behind Francis, who is sleeping with his head on his right hand, is the figure of Christ. St. Bonaventure recounts that Francis asked who the weapons were for and is told that they are for him and his knights. Christ further asks why he is more prepared to serve a servant than the God who is his master. Francis is then told to return home and wait for guidance as to what he should do.

4. *St. Francis before the Crucifix of San Damiano*
In this painting, Francis is praying before the Crucifix in the dilapidated church of San Damiano, where he hears a voice telling him to repair God's church – note the way this is expressed by the ruined roof on the top right. But as it turned out this was not a command for Francis just to rebuild San Damiano, but the whole Church.

5. *The Renunciation of his Worldly Wealth*
On the right is a semi-clothed Francis, having given back his own clothes to his father as a sign of the renunciation of his wealth. Bishop Guido of Assisi, a staunch supporter of Francis, can be seen wrapping him in his own cloak. The picture also expresses something of the outrage felt by Francis' father, depicted with his son's clothes over his left arm while his right arm is being restrained, as if he is preparing to strike out in anger. Notice that Francis' face appears to be turned not to his father but upwards towards God, symbolised by the remains of a hand extended in blessing.

6. *The Dream of Pope Innocent III*
The setting is the Basilica of San Giovanni in Laterano, Rome. The Pope has a dream of a poor man, of humble stature, none other than Francis indeed,

propping up the church with his shoulder to stop it toppling over. This is the first of the frescoes to portray Francis wearing his brown habit.

7. Confirmation of the Rule
Francis and his friars visit Pope Innocent III to ask his approval for the Rule of Francis and for permission to introduce this new Rule into the Church. The Pope's willingness to do so is demonstrated by his giving the sign of blessing over the kneeling Francis, so allowing him and his brothers to undertake the mission of preaching penance. In this picture Francis appears for the first time sporting a beard and the friars with him are tonsured, the traditional hair-style of Franciscan brothers.

8. Vision of the Flaming Chariot
The scene is believed to be set in Rivotorto, some distance from Assisi, where a number of the friars are shown either awake or sleeping, though Francis himself was in Assisi. Suddenly, in a vision, they are aware of the presence of Francis, who is being carried away in a magnificent Roman-style chariot of fire.

9. Vision of the Thrones
Once again we are in the presence of a vision. One of the friars is transported to heaven and sees a particularly splendid throne among other thrones. This throne was once occupied by the devil but is now reserved for the humble Francis. In the lower part of the scene the saint is praying before the altar and beating his breast. The angel indicates towards Francis with his right hand and towards the throne with his left.

10. Exorcism of the Demons of Arezzo
Above the city of Arezzo, Francis perceives many demons. He is kneeling in prayer and in front of him is his companion, Brother Silvester, standing at the city gate and who, when commanded by Francis, exorcises the demons and immediately they are gone.

11. St. Francis preaches to the Sultan
This is set during the Crusade of 1217–1221, which seemed to provide an opportunity for Francis to fulfil his longing to visit the Holy Land. To demonstrate the power of his faith Francis challenges the priests of the Sultan to walk through fire with him, but they are somewhat less than excited by the prospect! Francis points to the fire, a look of tranquillity on his face as someone who is willing to face the trial. Contrast this with the priests on the left who are shown scurrying away from Francis and the Sultan.

12. Ecstasy of Francis
Prayer was central to the life of the saint and in this fresco the friars witness Francis praying and at the same time being raised above the ground. He is

reaching towards heaven, his arms stretched out in the form of a cross, and is surrounded by a bright cloud. Christ is reaching down from the sky to bless him. Observe the look of astonishment on the face of his companions.

13. *Crib at Greccio*
In 1223, three years before his death, Francis wanted to reproduce in Greccio the scene of Christ's birth in Bethlehem as a means of assisting the worship of ordinary people and so began a tradition which still continues. The artist paints the event of the Crib in a church rather than in the open as Francis originally planned it. Dressed as a deacon, he kneels in front of the Crib while holding the Child. On the right Mass is being celebrated and the friars are singing!

14. *The Miracle of the Spring*
You will find this on the left-hand side of the main door. Francis is riding up a mountain on a donkey which has been loaned to him by a farmer who needs water to quench his thirst. To ease the man's distress, Francis gets down from the donkey and kneels in prayer, causing water to gush out from the rock. You can see the farmer crawling towards the spring to drink and the astonishment on the faces of Francis' two companions.

15. *Sermon to the Birds*
This is probably one of the most familiar episodes connected with St. Francis and can be found to the right of the main door. He is preaching to a flock of birds who show their response by flapping their wings, stretching their heads forwards, opening their beaks and touching his habit. Francis clearly understands that his ministry and mission mean reaching out to all God's creation.

16. *Death of the Knight of Celano*
A nobleman of Celano invites Francis to his home for a meal. Francis advises his host that he is soon to die and invites him to make his confession and put his affairs in order. The man does this and then suddenly dies while the others are at table. On the right side is the portrayal of the dead nobleman being held up by a woman, and Francis can be seen standing behind the table.

17. *St. Francis preaching before Honorious III*
Francis is preaching in front of Pope Honorious III. He is speaking on the left while one of his companions sits on the floor deep in thought, and the main part of the picture is taken up with the Pope and the surrounding Cardinals engrossed by what he is saying.

18. *Apparition at Arles*
On the left St. Anthony of Padua is preaching in the French town of Arles to the local Chapter of the Franciscan Order. Francis miraculously appears before them and extends his arms in blessing.

19. St. Francis receives the Stigmata

Here Francis, two years before his death, is praying on the slopes of Mount Verna and receiving the stigmata of Christ. From the figure of the Crucified Christ in the top right, rays emanate from his wounds and mark the body of Francis.

20. The Death and Ascension of St. Francis

At the moment of Francis' death a friar observes the soul of the saint being pushed up towards heaven by angels and enveloped in a white cloud. The lower part of the fresco shows the body of Francis surrounded by grieving friars, as well as by the clergy who represent the funeral rites.

21. The Apparition to Brother Agostino and Bishop Guido

As Francis dies, a friar named Agostino, sick, near to death and dumb, suddenly cries out for Francis to wait for him so that he can go with him. This is the scene on the left of the painting. Taking place at the same time, on the right, is a separate scene in which Bishop Guido of Assisi, on a pilgrimage in southern Italy, realises in a vision that Francis has died and is going to heaven.

22. Verification of the Stigmata

In an episode reminiscent of Doubting Thomas, a knight called Girolamo stops the cortege to verify the stigmata as the body of Francis is being taken from the Porziuncola to Assisi. The picture shows him touching the wound in Francis' chest. Above this scene is a large cross, and on the left is an icon representing the Madonna and Child, and on the right the Archangel Gabriel.

23. The Grief of the Poor Clares

As the body is being carried towards Assisi, the procession pauses at San Damiano so that Clare and her sisters may view his remains. The emotion of the occasion is portrayed by the nuns running out of the church to give him the last funeral honours. St. Clare, with the halo, bends over her spiritual father.

24. The Canonisation of St. Francis

On 16th July 1228, two years after Francis' death, Pope Gregory IX comes in person to canonise him and so officially declare him to be a saint. The solemn ceremony takes place in the Piazza del Commune in the presence of the friars, various dignitaries and the local people.

25. The Dream of Pope Gregory IX

Prior to the act of canonisation, Gregory appears to have had doubts about the veracity of Francis' stigmata. However, his fears are allayed when Francis appears to him in a dream and asks for an empty phial, which he then fills with blood from the wound in his side. Francis is standing behind the Pope's bed and hands the phial down to him, at the same time pointing to his wound.

26. A Man is Healed

The man is Giovanni from Lerida in Spain, who has been grievously wounded as the result of an ambush. Francis appears, undoes his bandages, lays his hands on him and the man is miraculously healed. The presence of the two angels symbolises the divine healing power.

27. Confession of a Woman restored to Life

This is a story about a woman who has died with an unconfessed sin. The angel of death soars over the scene ready to receive her, but is sent away by an angel. In the top left corner St. Francis is interceding on her behalf, so that she might be brought back to life and confess her sin to the priest who is by her bedside. This she does and then dies peacefully.

28. The Liberation of a Heretic

On the right is a dark dungeon in which a man named Pietro has been imprisoned for heresy. He appeals to St. Francis for help, who breaks his chains and sets him free.

The figure of Francis can be seen rising towards heaven, while in the centre of the fresco the Bishop is kneeling in prayer, recognising the miraculous intervention of the saint.

It is with this Life of St. Francis cycle that the 'Assisi Problem' presents itself at its most acute. Once more, but even more so than in the Lower Church, it raises the issue of Giotto or not Giotto? Up until the 1990s there seems to have been little questioning of Giotto and his school as creators of the cycle, but since then the matter has become one of the most controversial in art circles. Much of the debate centres on a different style of brush work in Assisi from other frescoes, for example in Padua, that are known definitely to have been by Giotto. However, if the frescoes in the Upper Church are not by Giotto, then by whom? Some experts now associate them with the Roman artist, Pietro Cavallini, though it might be a good idea not to raise too loudly doubts about Giotto in Assisi itself! Whatever the outcome of the debate, assuming it is ever satisfactorily resolved, what cannot be in doubt is that the paintings are by a genius who was not only a painter of great technical stature but someone who was also able to portray through art the humanity and naturalness both of St. Francis and those around him. Drama and simplicity are depicted side by side. Taken as a whole then, whatever the ongoing controversy about who painted what, the Basilica of St. Francis, both Lower and Upper Churches, is a most wonderful treasury of Italian art.

Leaving the Upper Church by the main exit brings you out to a lawn-covered piazza. From here you can look back and view the simple lines of the façade, with its large rose window surrounded by the symbols of the four evangelists. One final practical word about the Basilica – there is a strict dress code: shorts,

St Francis in its rural setting

mini-skirts or bare shoulders are not permitted, nor is the taking of photographs, and you are expected to remain silent.

OUTSIDE ASSISI'S WALLS

As with all tours, the time available determines how much of Assisi and its surroundings can be seen by the pilgrim. Many itineraries may include a day or half-day at the most. But for those visitors who are fortunate enough to spend longer here, especially those with a particular interest in St. Francis, there are three further sites just outside the city walls which merit a visit.

The first is the **Eremo della Carceri (The Hermitage)**, a delightful area of solitude nestling among the trees where Francis and his companions would withdraw for prayer and meditation. It is located some 2.5 miles outside the walls on the oak tree covered slopes of Mt. Subasio and not everyone who visits Assisi is aware of its existence. But be warned – the road is inaccessible to coaches or buses, so those who wish to visit must do so either by walking or by taxi. If you choose to walk then you leave the town from Piazza Matteotti and out through the Porta dei Cappuccini.

In the early 15th century St. Bernadino of Siena built a convent here and today it is occupied by a small number of Franciscans whose livelihood depends on alms, so a donation is most welcome. As with many religious sites you have to use your imagination to picture the original setting before the convent was built. The entrance to the Hermitage brings you into a courtyard and from this there is access to the refectory and the church. Among the various things you can see while visiting here are the grotto where Francis retreated to meditate and the rocky bed where he slept, an early, faded fresco showing him preaching to the birds, the hole through which it is said that he cast out a troublesome demon, and the ancient tree where, according to one tradition, he preached to the birds. If possible take time to explore the grounds, for their solitariness and peacefulness speak powerfully of the spirituality of the saint, and as much as anything else in and around Assisi, and perhaps even more so, the Hermitage is a particularly appropriate reminder of the true spirit of St. Francis.

The second is **San Damiano**, the little church where it all began for St. Francis and which was also central to the life of St. Clare. It can be reached by leaving from the Porta Nuova, turning right and taking the escalator down to the car park. Across from park is a path which will take you down to the church. Alternatively you can follow the sign from Via Vittorio Emanuele II. Again, for those who may find the walk difficult (remember, that having walked down you need to walk back up!) a taxi may be the answer.

In front of the church is a small piazza and entrance to San Damiano is through the Chapel of St. Jerome. Here you will see some valuable sixteenth century paintings by Tiberio D'Assisi. Then, follow through into the lovely and very simple church itself. Hanging above the altar is a replica of the Crucifix (now in Santa Chiara) from which Francis heard the command to rebuild the church. Dominating the church as it does, in your mind's eye you can picture what the scene must have been like on that dramatic occasion which was to change Francis' life and in turn, through him, that of Clare. In the apse is a choir dating back to 1504 and in the vault above the apse is a 13th century painting of the Madonna and Child in the company of St. Damian and St. Rufino. A door to the right of the altar leads to the very simple choir of the Poor Clares. If you climb a narrow staircase you will come to Clare's garden where it is believed that Francis composed his 'Canticle of all Creatures'. Also to be seen are the Dormitory where Clare and her sisters slept, the Cloister where they would have walked and the Refectory, still furnished with the original tables and benches, and where they would have eaten their meals in strict silence.

This, then, is where Francis brought Clare in 1212, and where she and her sisters were to spend their frugal lives in prayer and contemplation. Here they stayed until her death in 1253. As with the Hermitage, this simple and peaceful setting is a particularly fitting expression of the true nature of Francis' mission.

Even if time does not permit a visit to these two very special sites, then most groups will stop at the third one either on the way to or from Assisi. This is the church of **Santa Maria degli Angeli**, a short distance down in the plain below Assisi. From the outside it is what it appears to be – a large and imposing Basilica begun in 1569 and completed in 1679. An earthquake in 1832 caused much damage so that the nave and other parts had to be rebuilt. The present façade was the result of a further renovation in the 1920s. Though also damaged in the 1997 earthquake it has since been completely restored.

But however majestic it might appear from the outside, and there can be no denying its striking appearance, it is the interior which contains the building's gem. Once through the entrance you are immediately struck by a spacious, airy and relatively simple interior with a nave and three aisles. But as you move down the church its main purpose becomes clear, namely, to act as a protective shell for one of the most poignant symbols of St. Francis and the Franciscan movement, the *Porziuncola*. Standing beneath the dome this little

Santa Maria degli Angeli

chapel is where Francis retreated after forsaking the family wealth and where he founded the Order, later gathering his companions together here for the annual Chapter meetings. This, too, was where Clare received her habit from Francis and the Order of the Poor Clares was established.

This very ancient chapel belonged originally to the Benedictines, but having fallen into a state of disrepair it was renovated by Francis who then rented it from the Benedictines as a centre for his mission. The frescoes on the outside of the chapel are 19th century and replace previous ones. The painting on the upper part of the chapel's façade dates back to the early 19th century and its theme is the Assisi Pardon. This commemorates the indulgence Francis received from Pope Honorius III that each person who repented and confessed their sins should receive forgiveness on visiting the church of the Porziuncola. The Feast of the Pardon takes place each year from 1–2 August and pilgrims from all over Italy and the world flock to Assisi to celebrate it, though the indulgence extends to every day of the year. The interior is dark and simple, a place of peace and reverence. Behind the altar is a late 14th century polyptych by Ilario da Viterbo, portraying the Annunciation in the lower, central part and in the upper part Francis holding a rose crown up to Christ and Mary.

On the right of the Porziuncola as you walk towards the high altar of the Basilica itself is a doorway which can easily be missed and which takes you into the *Cappella del Transito*. This was the convent's infirmary where Francis requested that he should be brought for his last days and where he died on the evening of 3rd October 1226, 'naked on the barren ground'. Above the door on the outside of the chapel is a 19th century fresco by Domenica Bruschi illustrating Francis' death scene. On the inside walls are frescoes of some notable Franciscan saints and the first companions of Francis. A stone commemorates the place where the saint died and there is also a small 15th century terracotta statue of him.

As you leave here and walk back into the right transept you will see signs directing you to the *Rose Garden*. This small garden relates to a moment in Francis' life when, tempted by the prospect of the life he might otherwise have had, he threw himself into some rose bushes in the grounds of the Porziuncola as a physical penance. Tradition says that because of the blood which dripped from him due to the thorns, then all subsequent roses here have gown without thorns. Near here is the small *Cappella del Roseto*, the Chapel of the Roses, and Francis' own grotto from which he proclaimed the Pardon. The frescoes are by Tiberio D'Assisi and depict various episodes of the saint's life, including the proclamation of the Pardon.

A word of advice to the organisers of pilgrim groups would be not to rush Assisi. It is one of those places which rewards time spent in and around it, especially for those who want to savour something of St. Francis' captivating and challenging spirit.

Part 10
THE OTHER UMBRIAN SAINTS

While for many visitors to the region it will be St. Francis and St. Clare who attract most interest, it should not be overlooked that there are three other saints whose names are attached to this area – St. Benedict, St. Rita and St. Valentine. However, a pilgrim's particular interests and, of course, that old enemy time, will determine whether or not to venture beyond Assisi. But given an opportunity there is much to be said for exploring further.

ST. BENEDICT

Sometimes referred to as the 'Patriarch of Western Monasticism', the details of St. Benedict's life are somewhat sketchy and most of what is known comes from the biography of Pope St. Gregory the Great (c. 540–604), but even that is more a description of the saint's character rather than a factual account of his life. The bare bones are that Benedict was a twin, along with his sister Scholastica, and born at Nursia (c. 480) – present day Norcia – near Spoleto, in the declining years of the Roman Empire. The son of wealthy parents, he was duly educated in Rome. However, the permissiveness of contemporary society which he experienced there prompted him, though still a young man, to disengage from the world (c.500) and withdraw to a cave at Subiaco, where he lived as a hermit for some years.

Gradually a community of followers developed around him and he established 12 monasteries of 12 monks each, with abbots appointed by himself. But in due course (c. 525) local jealousy spurred him to move from Subiaco and, with a small band of monks, he went to Monte Cassino, remaining there until his death (c. 547). Soon after this move his sister, St. Scholastica, joined him at nearby Plombariola to found and govern a monastery of nuns. Fittingly enough they both died in the same year and within a short time of one another, and were buried together in the same tomb.

It was here at Monte Cassino that St. Benedict elaborated his plans for the reform of monasticism and composed his Rule. This was to become a blueprint for the monastic life and a singularly important document in Western civilisation. The Rule was created for people who wanted to live in a Christian contemplative community and consists of a prologue and 73 chapters detailing how to live a Christian life in a community of Monks or Sisters, and how a monastery should be organised and led. In drawing up the Rule, St. Benedict was much indebted to the rules of Basil, the Desert Fathers and Augustine among others. At this point it should be noted that Benedictine nuns, who were established by both St. Benedict and his sister St. Scholastica, live by this same Rule. Its aim is to balance prayer and work and this has been the ongoing principle of the Benedictines ever since their establishment. By becoming the foundation of the Western monastic movement, the Rule helped to spread Christianity, learning and civilisation throughout Europe after the fall of the Roman Empire. As such it would be difficult to under-estimate the importance and influence of the Benedictine Order.

Benedictines are not an Order in the same way as the Dominicans, Jesuits or Franciscans, i.e. under a central authority. Rather, they are a confederation of autonomous communities of men or women living under the authority of an Abbot or Prioress and following the Rule of St. Benedict. The unifying bond is allegiance to the same Rule. The principal monastery of the Benedictines is at Monte Cassino. Founded by Benedict himself around AD529, the monastery sits on a high hill overlooking the town of Cassino and the motorway between Rome and Naples.

It was totally destroyed by Allied forces in a series of bloody battles during the Second World War with over 100,000 American, British, other Commonwealth, Polish and German casualties, so that it has become a place of pilgrimage for that reason as well as for its place in the development of Christianity within Europe. The Monastery was rebuilt and re-consecrated in 1964. It should also be noted too, that as well as being important within Roman Catholicism, since the Reformation the Rule has also been significant within Anglican and other Protestant traditions. Nor should it be assumed that Benedictine monasteries are only for men or women. Indeed there are double monasteries, as among the Dominicans, where men and women worship together. Indeed, one such community exists at Burford in Oxfordshire where, in 1987, the Benedictine Priory welcomed men to join the community of women who had been there since 1941. This is an Anglican foundation where monks and nuns live in a joint community under the same roof and under the direction of an Abbott and a Prioress, working, praying and studying together, as well as offering hospitality to visitors who wish to spend time there.

Rising beneath the spectacular National Park of Monti Sibillini, present day **Norcia** is set in a wide plain and enclosed by a circle of medieval walls that still remain intact in spite of being badly shaken by various earthquakes. In the main square, the **Piazza San Benedetto**, is a statue of St. Benedict dating back to 1880, and facing on to the square is the 14th century **Basilica di San Benedetto**, built in the shape of a Latin cross and still maintained by the

Benedictine Order. Tradition says that this may be the site where Benedict and Scholastica were born, though an alternative view is that the crypt is built over the remains of an old Roman public building, possibly from the 1st century AD. There is a fine Gothic façade with a central rose window flanked by two niches containing statues of the twin Saints, though the Basilica was greatly modified later following earthquakes. The walls of the church are decorated with frescoes and paintings from the 16th and 17th centuries.

Also in the square is the 16th century **Castellina**, a papal fortress which now contains the civic museum. On display is a good collection of medieval wooden sculptures. Adjacent to the Castellina is the **Duomo**, the Renaissance Cathedral of Santa Maria Argentea (1560). In its time this also was a victim of Norcia's earthquakes, so that not much of the original survives, apart from the wooden doors which are still in place in the main doorway. Worthy of a visit, too, is the Gothic Church of *Sant'Agostino*, with its 16th century frescoes, including a well-preserved one of St. Augustine with the Madonna and Child. In addition, the *Oratorio di Sant'Agostinaccio* is notable for its fine inlaid, gilded and painted wooden ceiling, a masterpiece of local craftsmanship. Other churches are the 14th century church of *St. Francis*, with its rose window, and from the same century the church of *St. John*, with a finely decorated and carved altar from 1469.

ST. RITA

Also from Umbria was St. Rita (c. 1381–1457), born Margherita Lotti in the small village of Roccaporena near Cascia in the Diocese of Spoleto. Canonised on 24 May 1900, with her Feast day being 22 May, she was to become the Patron Saint of impossible causes.

The bald facts of her life are that from childhood she wanted to devote herself to the religious life and become a nun. Her parents, however, had other ideas and at the age of 18 she was pressed into marriage with Paolo Mancini. Various sources describe him as a strong and impetuous man, others as ill-tempered and cruel, but whatever the truth of his character and the problems she may have had with him, Rita behaved as an exemplary wife and mother for 18 years, repaying him with prayer and kindness. Some sources suggest that this brought him to repent of his behaviour. The marriage produced twin sons. Paolo, though, was murdered and Rita was anxious lest her sons should seek to take revenge for his death. As it was they both died within the same year before they could take the law into their own hands.

The death of her husband meant that she was free to follow her youthful sense of vocation – to enter the religious life and become a nun. However, when she sought admission to the Augustinian monastery of St. Mary Magdalene she was at first refused, but then later, so its is said, as a result of divine intervention, she was received and professed at the age of 36. She spent

Umbria – The green heart of Italy

the remaining 40 years of her life as an Augustinian nun, living a life of obedience and charity with great austerity. There is a legend that she so wanted to share the sufferings of Christ that, in answer to her prayers, her forehead became marked with a wound reflecting the crown of thorns. This she bore for 15 years, regarding it as a treasured gift.

Her symbol is roses, which are blest in Augustinian churches on her Feast day, 22 May. The tradition behind this is that during the last four years of her life she was confined to bed. A visitor from near her home enquired if there was anything particular she would like and her request was to receive a rose from the family estate. But as it was the month of January there was no hope of finding a rose and yet, however, a single rose was discovered blossoming from an otherwise barren bush.

Though believed to have once been a Roman settlement of some importance, **Cascia** no longer contains any evidence of its Imperial past. Today it is a pleasant town located in the most mountainous area of Umbria and near the Corno river. Venerated the world over because of St. Rita, many pilgrims come here to pay homage to her.

The *Basilica di Santa Rita da Cascia* was consecrated on 18th May 1947. Situated almost at the top of the old town, where access is assisted by escalators, it is built on the style of a Greek cross, with four large lateral apses and a dominant central cupola. On the main portal are sculptured episodes from the life of St. Rita, and her body, clothed in the habit of an Augustinian nun, is preserved in a glass case inside. Here, too, is the *Augustinian Convent* dedicated to her and where the nuns still live by the same rule as she did. The cloister of the convent is much as it was all those centuries ago. Important relics like her wedding ring and rosary are kept in the cell where she lived.

Other churches worth a visit in Cascia are the Gothic Church of *St. Francis*, particularly noted for its beautiful rose window; the Church of *St. Anthony Abate*, dating back originally to the 15th century, but reconstructed and modified during the Baroque era; the Collegiate Church of *St. Mary*, one of Cascia's oldest buildings, but also later modified as a result of earthquake damage, and displaying some impressive works of art, including restored frescoes from the 15th century; and the Gothic Church of *St. Augustine* with examples of frescoes from the Umbrian and Perugian schools.

Roccaporena is a village about three miles outside Cascia. Here it is possible to see the house where Rita was born, the Church of St. Montano where she married, the house where she lived after her marriage, and the garden in which it is said the miraculous rose was found. On the outskirts of the village is the *Sanctuary of St. Rita*, constructed in Romanesque style, and consecrated and first opened to the public in 1948.

ST. VALENTINE

Obviously, in popular awareness, St. Valentine is most clearly associated with Valentine's Day on 14th February. But who was he? Unfortunately, tying down his identity is not clear-cut an issue. Much of the story of St. Valentine is a mystery and the truth both about his identity and what made him special is obscured by centuries of myth and legend. Indeed, in 1969 St. Valentine was dropped from the liturgical calendar of the Catholic Church when it was decided to remove the feast days of saints whose historical origins were dubious! Nevertheless, given all the legendary accretions, there does appear to be some nucleus of fact.

Be that as it may, the Catholic Encyclopaedia cites at least three St. Valentines martyred on the 14th February. One is a 3rd century priest in Rome who was martyred c. 269 on the Flaminian Way under the Emperor Claudius II. Another is described as Bishop of Interamna (now Terni), who was taken to Rome and martyred round about the same time and whose remains were later conveyed back to Terni. The third lived and died in Africa and nothing else is now known about him. So, it is really the first two who concern us in trying to unravel this mystery. It could well be that the likeliest explanation is that they are both one and the same person.

So how did the name of St. Valentine become associated with courtship and love? Again, there is no shortage of explanations! Indeed, there are legends relating to both Valentine the priest and Valentine the Bishop. One such is that the Emperor Claudius II decided that single men would make better soldiers than married ones with their responsibilities for wives and families, so consequently outlawed marriage. The story continues that St. Valentine, conscious of the injustice of this decree, defied Claudius and continued to perform marriages for young lovers in secret. When this was discovered Claudius ordered that Valentine be put to death. Other stories suggest that Valentine may have been executed for attempting to help Christians escape from harsh Roman prisons. We really cannot be sure.

It has even been proposed that the Saint may have sent the first 'Valentine' himself! The story goes that while in prison he was visited by the jailer's daughter and that before his death he wrote her a final letter signed, 'From your Valentine'.

The association of the date of his death with 14th February is thought by some to be linked with romance because it sees the onset of spring and is said to be when birds select their mates. Or, the explanation may have something to do with the ancient Roman festival of Lupercalia, celebrated on 15th February, when a young man would draw the name of a young woman in a lottery to be his 'companion' for the year. Anyhow, whatever the truth in the legends, the Feast of St. Valentine was first declared to be on the 14th February by Pope Gelasius I in 496.

Present day Terni is very much the industrial centre of Perugia, having become part of the industrial revolution in the second part of the 19th century. Because of its production of iron, steel, chemicals, machinery, textiles and armaments, it was of extreme importance to the Italian war effort in World War II and, therefore, to the Allies who subjected it to heavy bombardment. As a result it suffered a great deal of damage and so the Terni of today is very much a modern city.

That said there are, however, some particularly impressive older buildings. There are the ruins of a 1st century Roman amphitheatre as well as the old town walls and various medieval houses. In addition there are a number of noteworthy churches – the Gothic church of **St. Francis**, with its very beautiful *Paradisi Chapel* decorated with 14th century frescoes; the ancient small church of **St. Alò**, a little treasure, dating back to the 12th century; **San Salvatore**, consisting of two adjacent buildings, one circular and the other rectangular, and featuring 15th and 16th century frescoes of the Last Judgement; the 13–17th century **Duomo**, begun in Romanesque style and completed in the 17th century Renaissance style, with a much prized wooden choir and a crypt dating back to the 11th century; and, of course, the 17th century **Basilica di Santa Valentino**, containing the saint's relics.

Part 11
ROME, ASSISI
and...?

For many organised pilgrim groups an 8-day tour, for example, of Rome and Assisi may be all that is required. On the other hand, there may be those groups which would like to include Rome and Assisi as part of a longer tour of Italy. This chapter aims to outline some of the possibilities for consideration.

FLORENCE in Tuscany is one possible add-on. It is a delightful city, picturesquely situated on both sides of the River Arnon and surrounded by the foothills of the Apennines. A city with a great artistic and cultural heritage it boasts such names as Dante, Michelangelo, Botticelli and Giotto among others. Nor should the considerable influence of the wealthy Medici family be forgotten, given that they played such a prominent role in the cultural rebirth of the Renaissance.

Though there is much to see and do in Florence, it is a very compact city so that most of what you may want to explore can be accomplished quite easily on foot. The wonderfully decorated **Duomo** which is one of the city's most prominent landmarks, the **Baptistry** where some of Florence's most distinguished citizens were baptised, and the **Campanile** are all favourites for visitors and if you have energy and a head for heights then a visit to the top of the Duomo or the Campanile provides wonderful panoramic views across the city towards the hills. The church of **Santa Croce** should also be seen, especially for the Giotto frescoes and the tombs of some of Italy's most famous men, among them Galileo, Machiavelli and Michelangelo, and so, too, should **San Lorenzo**, the parish church of the Medici family. The **Uffizi** is probably Italy's finest art gallery with the greatest collection of Renaissance paintings anywhere in the world. Nor will you want to miss Michelangelo's *David* in the Academy of Fine Arts.

A tour beginning in Florence can, for example, also take in nearby **Pisa** with its most famously known **Leaning Tower**. However, adjacent to this is the magnificent Pisan-Romanesque **Duomo**, with its striking four-tiered façade, and next to it the circular **Baptistry**. Time permitting, a visit to **Lucca** on the

Florence – The Duomo

way back to Florence is also highly recommened. The birthplace of Puccini, its narrow streets, medieval buildings and fine Cathedral of San Martino, make it an attractive proposition.

So, it could be possible to begin a tour in Florence and go either to Pisa and Lucca as a day excursion from there, or having explored Florence, drive down to Assisi but visiting Pisa en route, then staying overnight in or around Assisi. This would leave most of the next day to experience Assisi before continuing the journey to Rome in the mid-afternoon.

But if more is required then it could also be possible to begin such an Italian adventure even further north in wonderful **VENICE**, before then driving on to Florence, Assisi and Rome. Venice is a place about which the word 'unique' can justly be used. There is nowhere else quite like it, a magical city built on 118 small islands, whose streets are filled with water and traversed by almost 400 bridges. At the heart of the city is the **Piazza San Marco** in which is the majestic **Basilica di San Marco**, erected on the site of two previous 9th and 10th century churches and consecrated in 1094, making it Venice's oldest building. From floor to ceiling it is covered with glittering golden mosaics, the earliest dated from the 12th century, and depicting scenes from the Old and New Testaments as well as some particularly associated with St. Mark. Standing like a sentinel guarding the Grand Canal is the imposing Baroque church of **Santa Maria della Salute**, built in 1630 as a thanksgiving for the end of the devastating plague. Not to be overlooked either is the small and incomparable **Santa Maria dei Miracoli**, an early Renaissance masterpiece, or the huge Gothic church of **Santa Maria Gloriosa dei Frari**, the largest after St. Mark's, which among its works of art includes masterpieces by Titian and Bellini. In terms of art collections the **Accademia** contains paintings mainly by Venetian artists and provides an excellent overview of the Venetian schools from Byzantine to Baroque. In addition the **Peggy Guggenheim Museum** houses some fine 20th century paintings including works by Chagall, Dali, Kandinsky, Klee and Picasso.

Two of the city's most famous bridges are the **Rialto**, which spans the Grand Canal, and the **Bridge of Sighs**, which links the dungeons with the **Palazzo Ducale**, the home of the Doges who for nearly one thousand years were the city's rulers. If finances permit do have a drink in St.Mark's Square, where you can enjoy the orchestras and people watch, but be warned – prices are not cheap. Similarly a gondola ride may leave you thinking that you now have part ownership, but it is one of the things to do, part of the city's uniqueness, and it will enable you to see parts of the city that you might not otherwise discover, as long as you remember that a gondolier's hour is 50 minutes! A vastly cheaper alternative to a gondola, though much less elegant and romantic, is a *vaporetto* (water-bus) ride along the Grand Canal and from which you can see some 200 palaces in every style of architecture, especially the 15th century **Ca' d'Oro**, the most elegant Gothic palace in Venice. The journey gives an overwhelming impression of the city's wealth and splendour in its heyday.

An alternative extension to the suggested Venice and/or Florence possibilities could be to the south of Rome in and around **SORRENTO** and the stunning **Amalfi coast**, without doubt the most beautiful stretch of coast in Italy. Sorrento, with its magnificent views across the Bay of Naples towards Vesuvius, is a good base from which to explore this delightful area and a number of excursions are possible. A drive along the coastal corniche is an absolute 'must', a dramatic landscape of mountains, cliffs, coves and an enticing azure sea. Lovely towns dot the coastline: **Positano** clinging almost perilously to the hillside; **Amalfi** and its glorious **Duomo di Sant'Andrea** and lively piazza; **Ravello,** a charming hill-top village with picturesque gardens, churches and villas as well as matchless views of the coast.

From Sorrento you can also take a hydrofoil across to the island of **Capri**. With a wonderful climate it is something of an all-year round destination for visitors. Delightful little towns, spectacular scenery and a boat trip to the Blue Grotto all vie for the visitor's attention. So, too, do the designer shops in Capri Town!

But while in this area no one should miss an opportunity to visit **POMPEII** and **HERCULANEUM**. The story of the eruption of Vesuvius in AD 79 is well-

Herculaneum – with Vesuvius

Venice – The Grand Canal

known, when a massive explosion blew the top off the mountain and submerged both towns beneath pumice and ash. At the time Pompeii was a large, thriving, prosperous sea-port, whereas Herculaneum was a good deal smaller, never quite achieving the position of its more illustrious neighbour, but perhaps rather more select. Today, in terms of size, both sites reflect something of their past – Pompeii extensive, you could spend a whole day there depending on your energy levels, but you can still see a good deal in a half-day visit, and Herculaneum compact and very manageable as a morning or afternoon tour. Both retain some extremely well-preserved and colourful wall paintings.

These, then, are but suggestions about extending a basic Rome and Assisi tour. Indeed, it is perfectly possible within the compass of a 13/14 day tour to visit Venice, Florence, Pisa, Assisi and Rome, with a day excursion to Pompeii and Herculaneum. Such a tour may not come cheap, but it is most certainly highly rewarding. For many, though, Rome and Assisi may be all that is possible or necessary.

Part 12
LORETO

The hilltop town of Loreto (population 11,000) lies inland from the Adriatic coast, just south of Ancona. It is one of the most important shrines to the Virgin Mary for Catholics because it contains the tiny cottage, known as the Holy House, said to have been the house in Nazareth where Mary was brought up and in which she received the Annunciation. It would, therefore, also have witnessed the childhood of Jesus. Legend says that the house was borne away by angels in around 1291, after the Saracens had invaded the Holy Land in about 1249AD, and is believed to have arrived in Loreto in 1294, after a complicated journey with stops in Croatia and Recanti. The Santa Casa, as it is known, now lies beneath the great dome of the Sanctuario della Santa Casa, which dominates the town that has been built around it.

The late Gothic Basilica was begun in 1468, though it was not until 1507 that the Church, through the wishes of Pope Julius II, finally approved of Loreto as

Loreto – The Basilica of the Holy House   (Photo courtesy of Italian State Tourist Office – Fototeca ENIT)

a place of pilgrimage. The building is a mixture of Gothic and Renaissance architecture and contains the work of some of Italy's most celebrated artists and architects of the day. The octagonal dome was completed in 1500 and the façade from 1571–1587. This has a Madonna of 1583 by Lombardo, and magnificent bronze doors. The Santa Casa itself is surrounded by a 16th century marble screen with bronze doors, and inside, though blackened by centuries of candle soot, has 14th century frescoes and a cross. Over the main doorway is a life size bronze statue of the Virgin and Child by Girlamo Lombardo, and the richly decorated campanile has one huge bell weighing 11 tons. One of the great features of the Basilica is the number and quality of the frescoes that adorn it. Among the most important are those in the Sacristy of St Mark, by Merlozzo da Forli, and those by Signorelli in the Sacristy of St John.

Loreto has a great wealth of artworks, not only in the Basilica, but also in the 16th century Palazzo Apostolico which also fronts onto the Piazza della Madonna. Now known as the Palazzo Communale, it was designed by Bramante and contains an art gallery – the Museo Pinacotea. In the centre of the Piazza is a wonderful fountain dating from 1614, and there is also a statue of Sixtus V by Calagni, from 1587. The town also has a line of massive city walls which date from 1518, though they were later strengthened.

Florence – The Ponte Vecchio

Part 13
SAN GIOVANNI ROTONDO
The Shrine of Padre Pio

The incredible Story of Padre Pio, how at the age of 33 he received the stigmata, and how he carried the wounds, with blood always flowing from them, for half a century, but still carried on living the Life of a Capuchin Friar until he died in 1968, all this is well known and documented. He was clearly never a well man, often examined by doctors and cared for as a patient,

Having been ordained a priest in 1910 in the Cathedral of Benevento, he eventually came to the little town of San Giovanni Rotondo, in the Region of Puglia, on the "Heel" of Italy, where he arrived at the Monastery in 1916. It was two years later, as the First World Ward was coming to an end, that Pio received the five wounds of Christ upon his body before a large crucifix in the choir loft of the friary Church.

San Giovanni today is a town of some 21,000 people and is almost totally devoted to dealing with the seven million pilgrims who arrive each year. The focal point of their visit is the Church of Santa Maria delle Grazie, adjoining the Convent where Padre Pio worked as a priest. The much larger building close by is the Casa Sollievo della Sofferenza, or House for the Relief of Suffering, which Padre Pio caused to be built with the large amounts of money that flowed to him from all parts of the world.

Under the Church is the crypt, where the remains of Padre Pio lie in a marble tomb in an enclosure of wrought iron. It is always surrounded with fresh flowers. His cell can also be visited – it is kept as a museum with all his possessions

A huge, ultra modern Padre Pio Pilgrimage Church seating 6500 people was dedicated by Pope John Paul II in 2004. There is also a modern Way of the Cross built into the nearby hillside, which most pilgrims like to follow. It is built from granite with bronze and marble sculptures, and designed by the Sicilian sculptor, Francesco Messina

San Giovanni – The Shrine of Padre Pio (Photo courtesy of Italian State Tourist Office – Fototeca ENIT)

The statue of Padre Pio

(Photo courtesy of Italian State Tourist Office – Fototeca ENIT)

A number of miracle cures were attributed to Padre Pio which contributed to the lengthy process of beatification. In addition, he was widely believed to have a power of "bilocation", or the ability to be in two different places at the same time.

In 2008, his body was put on display in the crypt near his tomb to mark the 40th anniversary of his death. All the signs of the stigmata wounds had disappeared following his death, which is firmly regarded as another miracle, and Pio was finally canonized as a saint on June 16th 2002.

There is another important shrine, Monte Sant Angelo, just 14 miles to the east.

Part 14
FESTIVALS AND FIESTAS

Italians are as adept as any other people at the art of celebration – perhaps more so than most. And since most have a depth of religious conviction – which some of us might envy - they will often display their faith in the colourful and sometimes noisy processions with which they mark the major Christian festivals as well as the more locally significant saints days and other folklore displays which you will often find happening during your tour. It is always worth enquiring at the local Tourist Office to find out what is happening where you are – or perhaps you might look at the various websites – some of which we give below – before you leave home to help in planning your itinerary.

In Rome, as you would expect, Holy Week is celebrated in spectacular fashion with processions, passion plays and masses in all the great churches. On the evening of Good Friday, the Pope leads the procession of the Holy Cross from the Colosseum to the Forum and of course he will give the Blessing to the thousands of pilgrims gathered below from the balcony at St Peter's at noon.

The Feast of St Peter and St Paul is marked on June 29th with celebrations both in St Peter's and at St Paul Without the Walls, whilst on August 5th the Feast of Madonna della Neve is celebrated at St Maria Maggiore. Finally on December 8th there is the Feast of the Immaculate Conception marked by the Pope laying flowers at the Column of the Virgin in the Piazza di Spagna and Nativity scenes in many churches. Christmas starts with Midnight Mass almost everywhere, but especially in St Peter's with the Pope's Christmas Message given from his balcony.

Assisi's most special day is celebrated on May Day. Known locally as the Calendimaggio, it starts with a procession on the previous evening and there are processions of people in colourful medieval costumes with competing groups from the upper and lower towns. In fact May is a busy moth for festivals and fiestas throughout Umbria, most of them marking the return of springtime. The days of Whitsun and Corpus Christi are also the opportunity for religious festivals and these are sometimes marked by the laying of flowers - including a spectacular display at Spello near Foligno, in which the streets are covered with carpets of flower heads.

St Francis' own day is marked on October 4th, the date of his birth, which is also the anniversary of his death in 1226.

The Feast of the Pardon is marked on 1st and 2nd August and centres on the Porziuncola at Santa Maria degli Angeli. St Clare's birth is marked on August 11th and 12th, though the year may have been either 1193 or 1194.

We must also mention the celebrations surrounding St Rita at her birthplace of Cascia, the major events being held on May 21st and 22nd. On the first of these days there is a liturgical celebration followed by a candlelit procession and on the 22nd a historical procession with wonderful costumes. Orvieto also celebrates Corpus Christi in great style, but not all the festivals have a religious base. Several places in Umbria observe their own saints days in a rather more secular fashion – such as the Candle Race in Gubbio to commemorate their own patron saint, St Ubaldo, on 15th May. At Foligno a palio type horse race is run around the streets of the town on the 2nd Sunday in September.

For more information about events taking place, go the Local Tourist Offices (see pages 95–96) or visit the various websites:

www.tripadvisor.com/italy
www.alltravelitaly.com
www.umbriatravel.com with links to Assisi and other cities
www.festivalsinitaly.com with lists of festivals for each region.

The Monastery of Monte Cassino   *(Photo courtesy of Italian State Tourist Office – Fototeca ENIT)*

Part 15
THE PRACTICALITIES

GETTING THERE: Rome has two main airports – the main one, Fiumicino, also known as known as Leonardo do Vinci, is aprox 30km south west of the city, and has 2 terminals, one domestic and the other for international flights. Virtually all the scheduled flights arrive there. It has a direct rail connection with the Termini station in the city centre. The other airport is Ciampino, about 15km to the south east, which is used by most of the no-frills and charter airlines.

INTERNAL TRAVEL: Rome has an extensive bus network, including two lines of special interest to tourists – No 119 is an electric mini bus which covers the historical centre, whilst line 110 will give you a tour of the city on an open top double-decker bus, from Piazza dei Cinqueccento, near the Termini station. You can get a free bus map from the major bus stops. You need to buy tickets before you board – at tobacconists, bars and news kiosks - and date stamp them once aboard.

The Rome underground (COTRAL) has just 2 lines – Red and Blue. A third line is under construction. Maps prominently display the network outside every station. You can buy a book of tickets or a one day or weekly pass.

CURRENCY: The currency in Italy is the Euro. **Banks** with exchange offices (Cambio) are open from 0830 to 1320hrs, some main ones also from 1500–1630hrs. ATM's are everywhere to be seen.

ELECTRICITY: Standard current is 220v, 50Hz.AC. You will need a continental 2-pin adaptor.

EMBASSIES & CONSULATES: British Embassy: Via XX Settembre 80a Tel: 06 42200001. Eire: Piazza di Campitelli 3. Tel: 06 6979121. Australia: Via Antonio Bosio 5. Tel : 06 852721. Canada: Via Zara 30. Tel: 06 854442911. USA: Via Vittorio Veneto 121. Tel: 06 46741. New Zealand: Via Clitunno 44. Tel: 06 8537501. South Africa: Via Tanaro 14. Tel: 06 852541.

EMERGENCIES: The phone numbers are: Police – 113 for Municipal Police – the main emergency number: 112 for Carabinieri (for serious crimes). Fire – call

115. For medical needs call the first aid line (Samaritani) on 118; for Ambulance ring – 06-5510. There is also a general Tourist Help Line, which is 06-6712-052-28.

NEWS: Italian State Radio (RAI) has news in English Mon–Sat at 1000hrs, Sunday at 0930hrs

OPENING HOURS: Shops will usually open from 0900 to 1300 and 1530 to 1930 or 2000hrs. In the major tourist areas they may stay open for longer. Churches will usually close for a long lunch hour – probably 1230 to 1530 and may then re-open until 1800hrs. Museum opening hours vary considerably but the major ones may be open in summer until 10pm. Note that EU citizens over 60 can get reductions at most museums, and some transport facilities, by producing a passport.

PUBLIC HOLIDAYS: January 1st, January 6th (Epiphany) April 25th (Liberation Day) May 1st (Labour day) August 15th (Assumption Day) November 1st (All Saints Day) December 8th (Immaculate Conception) – as well as Christmas Day, December 26th, and Easter Monday. Local Saints Days are often also treated as public holidays.

RELIGIOUS SERVICES: For Catholics, Mass will of course be said at all of the churches you will visit, at times displayed on site. It will almost always be said in Italian, but there is an English Catholic Church – San Silvestro, at Piazza San Silvestro (Tel: 06 679 7775). The Anglican Church, All Saints, is at via del Babuino 153B (Tel: 06-3600-1881), and there is Methodist one at Via Firenze 38 (tel: 06-4747-36 75).

TIME: Italy works on Central European Time which is GMT + 1 and is thus normally one hour ahead of the UK. That means it is 6 hours ahead of New York but 8 hours behind Sydney.

TOURIST INFORMATION: There are offices of the APT at Via Parigi 11, at Termini Station and at the airports. In Assisi the Tourist Office is at Piazza del Commune, 22
The State Tourist Office (ENIT) is at Via Marghera 3 (Tel: 06-497-12 82)
The ENIT Offices outside Italy include those at:
London – 1, Princes St, W1R 8AY Tel: 020-7408 1254
Dublin – 47, Merrion Square, Dublin 2 Tel: 3531 766 397
New York – 630 Fifth Avenue NY10111 Tel: (212) 245-4961/4
Chicago – 500, N.Michigan Ave, IL60611 Tel: (312) 644-0990/1
San Fransisco – 360, Post Street, Suite 801, CA94108 Tel: (415) 392-6206

Sydney – Alitalia Office, Orient Overseas Building, Suite 202, 32 Bridge Street. NSW 2000 Tel: (2) 271-308 (also serves New Zealand)

Montreal – 1, Place Ville-Marie, Suite 1914, Montreal Que, H3B 3M9 Tel: (514) 866.76.67

Johannesburg – ENIT, London House, 21 Loveday Street, PO Box 6507. Johannesburg 2000 Tel: (11) 838-3247

For more information, including maps and Coming Events, visit the following web-sites:

www.enit.it   For UK: www.italiantouristboard.co.uk and for North America www.italiantourism.com

www. umbria2000.it – with links to Assisi and other Umbrian cities.

www.vatican.va – with English translation, good information and maps.

See also page 93.